The So...
Priorities for the Emerging Church

General Series Editor's Note

The Emerging Church series aims at fresh, positive and well-informed thought on some of the crucial issues for Christians today. The Church exists to do God's will in the real world and here some of its thinkers submit their ideas for renewal in spirituality, structures, worship and witness. They are not armchair critics but men and women who distil their experience and describe their vision for the Christian community, so that after thought and prayer, the Church may redirect its work for the sake of the Gospel in contemporary England. There is no time to lose. The history of prayer book reform, changes in the Church/State relationship and attitudes to reunion, show that about fifty years is needed in Britain for such proposals to be translated into practice. Discussion of the emerging Church of the twenty-first century is needed now.

An African bishop speaking to some English fellow Christians just before his country gained independence, said 'Remember, God is always ahead.' This conviction unites all these authors.

ALAN WEBSTER
Dean of St Paul's

The Scandal of Poverty:
Priorities for the Emerging Church

JOHN ATHERTON

MOWBRAY
LONDON & OXFORD

CONTENTS

Acknowledgements

I wish to thank a number of people who have helped in the writing of this book. Professor David Jenkins made important comments on the first draft with reference to theological matters, and my other colleague in the William Temple Foundation, the Revd Tony Addy, made suggestions regarding my handling of poverty. The editor of the Series, the Very Revd Alan Webster, and Canon Stephen Burnett were particularly constructive in their advice. Mrs Cleodie Mackinnon made the English more presentable and Mrs Kathleen Sheehan typed the various drafts. As is usual in such cases, my family bore the brunt of the burden involved in the production of a book in the midst of a busy life.

I have avoided the use of footnotes in order to allow people to wrestle with the argument itself. However, I have listed references from each chapter, along with books for further reading, at the end of the book.

INTRODUCTION

'I cannot help hoping and believing that before this generation has passed away we shall have advanced a great step towards that good time when poverty and wretchedness and human degradation which always follow in its camp will be as remote to the people of this country as the wolves which once infested its forests'.

David Lloyd George, 1909.

Belief, however powerfully expressed, needs to be sustained by more than firm hopes if it is to be translated into effective policies. Nearly seventy-five years after Lloyd George made his declaration of war against poverty and squalidness, both continue to cast their dark shadow over British society. Hypothermia among the elderly, the growing incidence of child-battering and increasing unemployment face us with a deeply human predicament affecting many millions of our people which requires a response from each of us as ordinary men and women.

Poverty and what it does to *all* people, whether poor or rich, is one of today's most disturbing problems. More clearly than any other issue, the plight of the poor calls us to move to a fundamental reappraisal of our view of society and what it means to be human. The question of poverty and our response to it is a key test of the moral adequacy of ourselves, our governments and any emerging Church.

1

Writing in a pamphlet on the London poor in 1883, the Congregationalist, Andrew Mearns, described the supreme importance of the poor for the Church in powerful words: 'There is no more hopeful sign in the Christian Church of today than the increased attention which is being given by it to the poor and outcast classes of society. Of these it has never been wholly neglectful; *if it had it would have ceased to be Christian*. But it has, as yet, only imperfectly realized and fulfilled its mission to the poor.'

Because the issue of poverty is so grave a matter, it must not be allowed to become yet another issue on the indiscriminate agendas of the Churches. This book has therefore been written to make more widely available to the Churches and beyond some of the thinking and practices emerging in the great and continuing debate over poverty. The Church cannot remain aloof from that debate. Facing up to the facts about poverty raises such fundamental questions about our very humanity that it will drive us to discover what it must mean to be the Church in the last decades of the twentieth century. That is a possibility of great hope for people and Church.

PART ONE

What it Means to be Poor: Why the Churches must be Involved in the Question of Poverty

CHAPTER ONE

What is it Like to be Poor in Affluent Britain Today?

Any adequate understanding of poverty should begin and end with a consideration of what it means to be poor. It should never be forgotten that being poor is the whole life-experience of men and women like ourselves. It is far more than a 'problem for investigation, classification and report.'

It is important to listen to the poor describing what poverty is like. At the heart of the predicament of the poor is the fact that they are never listened to; they do not have a voice. The theologian Ronald Gregor Smith noted that the greatest danger facing people today is 'the fearful assumption that man is there to be managed.' To this general threat the poor are particularly vulnerable. Having no voice in government, in the trade unions, in the educational and health services, or in the Church, their fate is to be neither seen nor heard.

The aim of this chapter is to provide a picture of what it means to be poor in our affluent society. It will do this by sharing the experience of four groups of people who are particularly vulnerable to poverty, and by looking in contrast at the experiences of the affluent.

FOUR EXPERIENCES OF POVERTY

The One-Parent Family: Mary and her Kids
Mary is in her thirties, divorced, with three children aged three, seven and twelve. She lives in a house set in a row of average-quality terraced housing in a small industrial town in the Midlands. Since her children are still rather young she thinks it necessary to stay at home and look after them, even though she would prefer to be at work earning reasonable money as a qualified secretary. She is totally dependent upon supplementary benefit for her income, and has no assets other than £5 in the Trustee Savings Bank for each of the children.

Behind the ordinary respectable front which the outside world sees, there is a very anxious woman struggling to make ends meet on all fronts of the family's life. Food, clothing and heating are particularly expensive. For years she has neither bought any new clothes, nor had her hair done. The children manage with good second-hand clothes, though even this is not easy because they wear and grow out of them so quickly. In a revealing moment Mary commented: 'I don't manage to get meals during the day. You wonder where your next penny is going to come from. Bills, how to pay them, how to clear one before the next one comes... Clothes are always a worry... I'd like to live a normal life, but can't afford it, especially in winter when we can't afford coal.'

Mary understands only too well that whatever else education is supposed to be it's certainly not free. It's not only all those 'extras' which mean so much to children that she can't afford—the school photograph, field trips, visits to places of interest and holidays. Increasingly she is being asked to buy additional books and expensive sports equipment. It's even worse in the school holidays when she has to find money for all their meals, treats, and additional wear and tear to their clothes and shoes. Leisure is not a period of refreshment but is the cause of greater anxiety: 'I dread the holidays because of our financial situation.'

6

So often the routine of life is made tolerable by the purchase of ordinary household goods; yet Mary is frequently not able to buy washing-up liquid, washing powder, toothpaste and newspapers. 'We find it hard. One toothbrush manages twelve months and we don't have one each always, but really could do with one every three or four months'. The unexpected makes the burden even more unbearable. A sister's funeral can impose a crippling extra burden of £9 for a wreath, and £3 for bus fares. Under all these pressures she can never plan ahead. She can only live from day to day, dreading the week's money running out. To survive always means going without food or heat, running up fuel and rent debts and borrowing.

The effect on Mary of the sheer struggle to make ends meet both creates and is made worse by her isolation from the social life of friends, family and neighbourhood. She always feels 'trapped in the house' because she never has enough money 'to get a bus to visit the family'. That isolation was turned into total rejection when she fell victim to the drive against social security scroungers in the town. She was accused of cohabitation and lost her supplementary benefit. Fortunately, with the help of the local welfare rights organisation, she managed to prove that the suspect was her brother-in-law, but not before she was visited first by investigators, and then by the police in a panda car, and had been interrogated three times at a social security office.

For Mary it's not the social stigma of poverty or the hardship of life on social security which hurst most. It's rather knowing what you and your family are deprived of compared with everyone else. It's 'being embarrassed and having to humiliate yourself when you go to someone else's home and see what they have got and they come to your home and they see what you have got. I feel as if I cannot invite other people home . . . If I could just buy the little luxuries for my kids that other kids get. If Debbie asked for chops and I could go out and get them. We've never seen chops in this house and Debbie wants trousers and a top . . . like her mates. But I can't afford it . . . I am always under stress because of trying to make ends meet and not being able to do right by the kids . . . It's the little things that hurt most. The curtains are over five years old. Food mostly has to be beefburgers, chips and eggs. Children cannot have toys. I think the hardest things are lack of clothes and nice crockery. Walking by shops with nice clothes in the windows makes me feel sick. I can't go out often as I have no money.'

In 1971 there were 601,000 one-parent families with 1,066,000 children.

In 1980 there were 920,000 one-parent families with over 1,500,000 children.

49 per cent of the families and 59 per cent of the children are in or on the margins of the State's poverty line.

Mike, Ann and the Kids: The Long-Term Unemployed

Mike and Ann are in their early twenties with two children aged two and six. They live in the inner urban area of one of the great industrial cities in the North West. Although Ann works in a pub for two evenings a week, she does not declare her tips to the social security office. The family is dependent on supplementary benefit for the bulk of its income.

Mike and Ann feel fortunate to have rented a poor terraced house from the Council. The house is situated in a twilight inner city area, has four small rooms, a tiny kitchen, an outside WC, and no bath or cooker. There is one cold water tap. Even with a blazing coal fire the house is cold, which is not surprising since the roof leaks and the doors and windows fit badly. Because of the dampness and the draughts it has proved impossible to free the house of cockroaches and bugs.

Mike is one of the growing number of those who have been without work for over twelve months. Over two years ago, despite poor health, he got a job labouring in a factory which had secured a good export order. He got his cards when the order wasn't repeated and so the firm cut back. He obtained no redundancy money and since his wages were never good, earnings-related unemployment benefit was of no use to him. And, having always lived between low-paid jobs and unemployment, he has no savings. With the competition from thousands of other unskilled people now joined by the army of unemployed youngsters, he has no chance of getting a job.

After fourteen months without work, and dependent on the lowest rate of supplementary benefit, Mike's belief in himself has been virtually destroyed. Apathy and fatalism are punctuated with his aggressiveness particularly against Department of Health and Social Security officials, but this only invites harsher treatment from them. He feels and acts like a defeated victim whose fall has brought down with him the entire family group. Marginal to society, irrelevant to the world of work, he is quite powerless to change his situation.

What makes his unemployment worse is the stigma people and society attach to it. Standing in long queues at Unemployment and Social Security offices is a humiliating experience especially when an anti-scrounger campaign is on the public rampage. The effect of such sustained campaigns has coloured his family's life and their relations with neighbours and friends. 'People look on us as scroungers . . . we feel so ashamed, so low, as if we are beggars'.

As if this were not more than enough for any family to bear, there is always the major nagging worry over money. 'The real problem' for Mike 'is making ends meet. To have to set a budget and stick to it. When I was working, the extra £20 or so made all the difference'. Yet, despite the continuing threat to sanity of subsistence living, they are efficient managers given their appallingly limited resources. Ann always pays the bills because we're 'afraid to get into debt, but we've often had to miss food to do it'. Feeding the family is a titanic struggle. 'It takes two of us three or four hours each week working out what we can afford to buy in just food. We are tied to a monotonous routine regarding food . . . On the money you get it is impossible to make ends meet. You have to have the cheapest food. The same food week in week out. I get sick of it'. Nutritious and commonly consumed food like cheese, fresh vegetables, fruit, meat, butter, fish, biscuits, and cereals are rarely part of their diet.

Fuel bills and the cost of the kids are major headaches, and the family increasingly gets into arrears with the former. With the latter, 'Clothes are always a worry', especially for fast-growing children, and so they are all dependent on second-hand clothes. Yet even at six years old, the 'eldest child hates wearing second-hand clothes'. School outings for her are out, of course. Where do you find £2.50 to go on a school trip if you live on supplementary benefit, even though you earn a bit on the side? Christmas and birthday presents and parties are either not on or are dependent on the generosity of relatives.

In the midst of all this struggle to survive, and even though Ann and Mike were always up against it, they gave away a table, chairs and dresser to a neighbour worse off than they were.

> In January 1982, 905,100 people had been unemployed for over twelve months (29 per cent of the unemployed).
> In April 1975, 135,600 had been unemployed for over twelve months (12.8 per cent).

Jim, Barbara and the Kids and especially Dave: the Large Family

Jim and Barbara, with their four children, live on a large council estate in London. Boasting one pub, one church, and few other facilities, the estate is geographically isolated, and presents a spartan treeless front to the outside visitor. Because it has a bad name, it is not easy to get credit, and the authorities fight a losing battle against vandalism. Jim and Barbara's three bedroomed semi was built in the early fifties, and although it has a back garden it's really an area of bare soil strewn with rubbish and broken toys. Inside the house the environment is equally unattractive. 'The rooms are damp and the children have bronchitis (in one room it was so damp that it stripped itself)'. The underfloor electric heating system is very expensive and not really adequate in winter, a problem not helped by a broken bedroom window. Poor furnishings add to the impression of near-destitution. The furniture is old, dirty and rickety; the mattresses are soiled and smelly; there are fewer than one pair of sheets and three blankets for each bed, a shortage made up by the use of old clothes and not helped by the sight of van loads of blankets leaving Britain for the Italian earthquake zone, some only to be left to rot in some foreign field. The family is well aware that it has no capital or assets. 'There is nothing we own which would fetch a decent price'.

Jim is a low-paid general labourer with a history of probation, detention centres, absenteeism at school, and intermittent unskilled employment. When he found out that Barbara was pregnant with their eldest child, Dave, they decided to marry. (Jim was twenty-one, Barbara seventeen). Several miscarriages and three children under seven later, Barbara looks in her fifties (she is in fact in her early thirties), and suffers from varicose veins and high blood pressure. Exhaustion, depression, repeated pregnancy, and resentment at being kept short of money mean that she has lost all interest in sex. Their relationship is increasingly turbulent with continual rows occasionally breaking into violence. While Jim seeks relief in smoking and frequent visits to the local pub, Barbara is left with the task of keeping the house and family going. Her daily chores include getting two full lines of washing out of an old machine, sweeping the floor (she has no vacuum cleaner), washing three young children, and feeding six mouths. Since she gets no help from Jim, and since three of the children wet their beds regularly (they have no rubber sheets), it is not surprising that the children are often dirty and their clothes grubby. In no way can she hope to keep up with things, and in the last few years, she has only twice allowed herself the compensation of spending money on herself.

Inevitably, the relationships of parents and children are constrained by poor diets, lack of sleep, polluted air, ill-health, and all the extra stresses of financial harassment. The home is dominated by the noise of children fighting, Barbara shouting and the TV blaring. Faced with these pressures, both parents, after initial firmness, give in to the children for the sake of peace, changing easily from wielding the stick to offering the carrot. The children always therefore feel at the mercy of unexplained arbitrary and illogical rules. They rapidly become as physically and verbally agressive as their parents.

For a large family dependent either on a low-paid worker or on supplementary benefit, their income is never sufficient to meet their basic needs for food, clothing, heat and occasional crises. Their diet is sparse and dull, rarely including coffee, jam or cakes, and dangerously cutting back on high protein foods like meat, fish, cheese and eggs. Given Barbara's anguish at watching the children go without food, their aim is to satisfy hunger through bread, potatoes and watered milk; it is never to provide a balanced diet. Eating for such a low paid, large family therefore takes the following shape on a typical day:

Adults	Children
Breakfast – coffee, toast.	Breakfast – cereal.
Lunch – nothing.	Lunch – school dinner.
Tea – spaghetti, bread, margarine, jam.	Tea – spaghetti, bread, margarine, jam.
Supper – tea.	Supper – tea and sandwich.

Clothing is almost always second-hand, with the children causing the main headaches. Indeed, so bad did the situation become that the children were kept off school because they no longer had even their normal footwear of plimsolls. For Barbara, 'school clothing problems are the worst as the children can't go to school without proper clothes'. Even though they are often cold, and so go to bed early, they are always in trouble with their fuel bills, currently owing over £100, and they have had their electricity cut off three times. The inevitable occasional crisis just doubles their already unbearable burden. A £2.80 taxi bill to take the youngest child to hospital in the middle of the night can only be found from the rent money, since they have no savings to fall back on. In these circumstances, Christmas becomes a matter of buying a piece of lean bacon and boiling and roasting it. 'It cost £1 but it was worth it . . . My husband's sister bought a Christmas present'. Birthday parties are out except on a strictly controlled rota system. 'We only have a birthday recognized every three years as we can't afford presents'. For once in their lifetime, the whole family saved up for a holiday last year—a trip to the local cinema with ice cream at the interval. Apart from this, there has been no socializing as a family, no entertaining, no visiting friends and relatives. 'We keep ourselves to ourselves' and pay the high price of 'my older son, seventeen, having to make excuses to his friends about not going out with them in the evenings and weekends because he doesn't want them to know how poor we are'.

Faced with all these cumulative pressures, the family can only keep going by either running up debts or leaving bills unpaid. It is always one or the other. The result is that keeping creditors at bay becomes almost a full-time job of the most draining kind. There is never any chance of planning ahead; their concern is always with the present. Their expectations for themselves and for their children are at best low-paid employment, at worst unemployment.

That expectation has been realised in their eldest son. Dave is nearly eighteen. He left his local secondary school nearly two years ago. Because he was away from school most of his last year with rheumatic fever, he did not take any examinations. He showed no signs of those cues and stances which outside institutions interpret as meaning the possession of ability. When he left school, he would have liked to become a chef, but his first job, which he found himself, was working in a local warehouse. After he had been there for about two months, he had a blackout. The manager said he was obviously not suited to heavy

13

work and sacked him. After two months on the dole he got another job in another warehouse, but when he returned after a few days' illness the manager refused to accept the sick note and dismissed him. He has not been employed since. Although he has tried to get a job by every way he can think of, he has had no luck so far. Asked what he will do if a job does not turn up soon, he can only shrug his shoulders. Dave wants to work in the neighbourhood, and would take any job offered but is not very interested in what he gets: 'a job's just a job, isn't it?'

In 1977 3,910,000 families out of 25,530,000 had income below or at the supplementary benefit level. They included 1,420,000 children.

In 1977 there were 421,000 large families with four or more children. Approximately 20 per cent lived at or below the supplementary benefit level.

In 1982 230,100 of the unemployed out of 3,070,600 were aged between sixteen and eighteen years (7.5 per cent).

Mr and Mrs Brown: The Elderly

Mr and Mrs Brown live in a beautiful village in the South East. Their house, a rented four-roomed cottage, has no mains sanitation or bath, and has an outside WC. They have no fridge, washer or TV, but do own a radio. Their furniture is old and simple, but well kept.

Totally dependent on the old age pension, they only keep out of debt by concentrating their spending on the rent, fuel and food. They have rarely anything left at the end of the week for clothes and leisure activities. Although they have managed to save £215 over a long life-time of agricultural labouring, they are still below the official state poverty line and so are entitled to supplementary benefit. Along with 560,000 pensioners (excluding wives and dependents) they are too independent and proud to claim it. Fortunately, they manage to grow some of their own vegetables, but their health is none too good and so they will not be able to rely on this additional resource for much longer.

Fuel and food are their major problems. Having no transport, they are compelled to shop locally, and this is always more expensive than the supermarkets in the neighbouring market town. Buying only a little at a time, since they have no freezer or fridge, also adds to the cost of eating. It is not surprising that Mrs Brown could say that 'the last time I had a good meal was when I was in hospital'. Yet even the meals on wheels service is being cut back.

Keeping warm is a continuing struggle, especially in winter (at least 700,000 old people are at risk from hypothermia each winter). Their only heating is a single-bar electric fire; yet even this is increasingly expensive since gas and electric prices went up by 30 per cent in 1980 and 25 per cent in 1981. 'We both get very cold at times', Mrs Brown says, 'and have to go to bed early evenings to get warm, which is not really a good thing for us'. Although they wear gloves, hats and socks in order to keep warm in the house, they have not as yet resorted to putting layers of newspapers between the blankets and cracks in the floor.

Perhaps Mr and Mrs Brown's gravest deprivation is their enforced isolation. Having no transport of their own they are totally dependent on others to get out of the village. Visits to relatives and to the market town for their pension and for personal and household goods have to be planned well ahead. Since they are not on the phone, messages have to be got to their son and daughters, the nearest of whom lives fifteen miles away (local children cannot afford the prices of houses in the village because of the competition from second-home buyers from the cities). Following economy drives by the area transport authority, there has been no bus service for years. There is a strange irony in the Browns' fate. As they sit imprisoned in their front room or garden, they watch the hordes of holiday visitors who descend on the picturesque village in their cars and coaches and then drive off again. The Browns, who helped to create the village and feed the visitors, remain virtually stuck in their own garden. And they feel their deprivation and accept it.

In 1911 there were fewer than 3,000,000 people of pensionable age.

In 1975 there were 9,500,000 people of pensionable age. 20 per cent of these lived in poverty (36 per cent of the poor in the UK are elderly).

THE AFFLUENT

Poverty is about more than being poor. Running through the four pictures of what it means to be poor is the sharp awareness that poverty is also about not being like other families. It is about being deprived of what so many in our society take for granted. What the poor miss most are the ordinary things of life so intimately associated with the 'normal standard of living' powerfully presented through the media. They miss taking the children to the seaside in 'the age of the train' and the car. They long for a good meal with a joint, two veg. and a sweet. They would love to have a full pantry. They are deeply aware of all the consequences for daily living of not being able to put a bit aside for a rainy day. As Mary observed, poverty is about going to someone else's home and seeing what they have got and then going to your home and seeing what you have not got. So much of the problem of poverty is to do with its existence in an affluent society.

What is affluence? What is life like on the other side of the coin to poverty? A brief glimpse into the lives of the affluent completes the picture of what it means for the families of Mary, Mike and Ann, Jim and Barbara, and Mr and Mrs Brown to be poor in affluent Britain today. Of course, by the affluent is not simply meant the really rich, those who cluster together in places like Eaton Square in London's West End. Out of its 230 households, over fifty are represented in *Who's Who*. Using their flats in the weekdays, they spend their weekends and summers in their country houses and abroad. They represent an intricate network of ties by blood relationship and marriage, cemented by 'interlocking directorships in banking, insurance, industry and commerce'. Between them they own a considerable proportion of the nation's wealth, were educated at the major public schools and Oxbridge, and use the same exclusive clubs like White's.

The Sunday Times colour supplement 'A life in the day of' series vividly described what the experience of the very rich can mean. 'I wake up sometimes and think "Oh God, another day of decisions" and maybe go back to sleep for another half-hour. You know: where are the children going to spend their holidays? So-and-so's coming into London: are we going to give a dinner, cocktails, a party? What? Are we going to fly to California? Am I supposed to be going to Paris? All those things'. We later learn from the article that the writer, who lives in London, has an apartment in New York, a house in Jamaica, land on Mustique, and was off to California in a couple of days to buy another house.

Such families are the really rich in society. Far more are wealthy in a more ordinary kind of way, and are to be found in most areas of the country. Peter Townsend describes the experiences of two such families in the following way: '*Mr and Mrs Margood*, both aged thirty-five, live with two daughters and two sons aged from three to eleven near a small town in Kent. The house has eight bedrooms, is in several acres of ground', and is estimated to be worth nearly £90,000. His father was a highly skilled manual worker, hers a barrister, and they met at university. He is an economist in an insurance company earning over £16,000 per annum, with over six weeks holiday a year and a pension of two-thirds his final earnings at sixty. Through the Company he pays only 3.5 per cent interest on his mortgage, and they have an income from their shares, family trust, and bank deposit account of over £30,000 before tax. They also have overdraft facilities. All the children are being educated privately, both parents have cars, and they do a lot of entertaining.

17

Mr and Mrs Avis-Brown, sixty-two and sixty, live in a detached house with a large garden in Surrey estimated to be worth over £50,000, to which they moved on Mr Avis-Brown's retirement as a bank manager two years previously. He receives a pension of over £8,000 per annum, along with over £2,800 in dividends and interest. They have a car, and they entertain and go out to dinner two or three times a week. Their house is beautifully furnished and contains valuable silver and pictures.

When asked whether there was any real poverty these days, both families said there wasn't any because there was always supplementary benefit to fall back on.

Conclusion

These are some of the experiences of what it means to be poor and wealthy in the same affluent society. Each story represents lives being lived in a nation reigned over by the same Queen. Yet, like the young stranger in Disraeli's *Sybil* we are driven to ask 'Which nation?' As in 1845, the stories of our families are the stories of life in 'Two nations: between whom there is no intercourse and no sympathy; who are as ignorant of each other's habits, thoughts and feelings, as if they were dwellers in different zones, or inhabitants of different planets; who are formed by a different breeding; are fed by a different food; are ordered by different manners, and are not governed by the same laws'. To examine what this great gulf means for the poor and therefore for our society and all its members is the aim of the rest of this book.

CHAPTER TWO

Why Take the Poor Seriously?

'It's impossible to live in poverty today.
You are given enough for food and rent.
What makes people poor is buying fags
and booze. It's their own doing. There's
no such thing as poverty'.
Mr Dibshoss, 45, Company Director.

It is easy to think of obvious reasons why the poor should
be taken seriously after the summer of 1981. The riots in
Brixton, Liverpool 8 and Moss Side and the growth of
large-scale long-term unemployment are the kind of signs
of the times which people ignore at their peril. Yet it is
more important to begin an enquiry much lower down the
stream with what people *actually feel and believe* about
poverty. In the face of growing social conflict and
unemployment, it is natural to assume that everyone will
be concerned about such problems. Yet the truth of the
matter is very different. Many see the poor through the
eyes of Mr Dibshoss, believing that there is no such thing
as poverty and, even if there were, that it would be the
poor's own fault.

1. What People Feel and Believe About Poverty: Perceptions and Attitudes.

So many either do not believe poverty really exists, or if
it does then it must be the poor's own fault, that these
perceptions and attitudes become important parts of the

reality and problem of poverty. Yet, like poverty itself, people's perceptions and attitudes about the poor are concerned with more than poverty. The poor themselves are made more aware of their poverty by their life within an affluent society. Looking at what is meant by poverty should therefore include a consideration of what people feel about equality and inequality in British society. For Christians an enquiry into what people actually see and believe about poverty is particularly important. Concerned as they presumably are with getting at the truth of the matter, they need to begin not with grandiose views about Christian solidarity with the poor but rather with the recognition that they themselves are intimately involved with commonly-held perceptions and attitudes about poverty. Only after a self-examination as to what they really feel and think about the poor in the light of these commonly-held perceptions and attitudes will they be in a position to probe into both the reasons why the poor must be taken seriously and how this will affect their own views.

Perceptions of Poverty.

> 'There's still rich and poor people but not very many. I feel sorry for those aristocrats having to sell their estates'.

The comment of this old-age pensioner living on supplementary benefit illustrates how one of the greatest obstacles facing the poor is the fact that so many people simply do not believe that they exist. They do not see any poverty in our society.

In Peter Townsend's great survey at the end of the 1960s, over one-third of those interviewed, including many who were poor themselves, did not believe that there was any such thing as real poverty; the existence of poverty is widely denied and not least by its victims.

In the light of such ignorance it is not surprising that people have inaccurate views of who the poor are. When asked who they thought were likely to be poor in today's society most said the elderly. They ignored the growing army of three million unemployed and the fifty per cent of single-parent families who are totally dependent on supplementary benefit. Low-paid workers similarly were not seen by themselves or others as being in poverty. People could not see beyond the obvious and deserving elderly to the bulk of the poor who are less obvious and frequently regarded as undeserving.

This lack of clarity about the existence and nature of poverty is only increased by people's propensity to believe that they are all in the same boat. Like Mrs Thatcher's reply in 1978 to the comment of a woman carpetmaker that she couldn't afford to buy one, people tend to plead, 'My dear, we are all poor' these days, even when many are obviously affluent and many are obviously poor. Confusion over the reality of poverty is only exacerbated by confusion over the reality of equality. Both are ways of getting off the hook because they are never grounded in the truth of the matter. Both spring from a refusal to face up to the true nature and extent of poverty. Both are derived from false perceptions of poverty and what is going on in society.

Attitudes to Poverty.

> 'People are poor because they've never appreciated the value of money; they've never looked ahead. They go out drinking when they've got it with no thought for the future'.

This statement by a 56 year old machine operator confirms that the way people see poverty is strongly influenced by their attitude to the poor. And like their perceptions, their attitudes are often neither very accurate nor very moral. In a recent survey of what people thought were the causes of poverty, the biggest number said that poverty was caused by financial mismanagement. Wasteful spending, too much HP, the refusal to save, and imprudent breeding habits lay at the root of the predicament of the poor. It was their failure to control the money going out of the home, and not society's refusal to allow more to go into the home, which was the cause of their problem. Even when unemployment reached three million, many still felt that the unemployed were lazy and could get work if they tried harder. Their dependence on supplementary benefit was regarded as sponging on society. It was all a matter of blaming the victim.

The widespread and deep-rooted attitude to the poor which sees their predicament as their own fault is confirmed from two other sources. The British rarely come top of any league these days. But in a recent Common Market survey they came top by a mile of the 'defective attitudes to the poor' league! Of the British interviewed, 43 per cent thought the main cause of poverty was laziness or lack of willpower. This contrasted with an average among all the remaining member states of 25 per cent so explaining the existence of poverty.

The blaming-the-victim approach to poverty is not surprisingly also reflected in negative attitudes to social security. If the poor are poor because it's their own fault, then inevitably people will say that benefits are too high for the likes of them. Surveys have revealed that six out of ten said benefits were too generous and too easy to get, four out five said too many depended on welfare, and two out of ten said welfare made people lazy.

It is on these defective attitudes that Government builds its policies against the scroungers and Fleet Street sells its newspapers. And because it is the actual perceptions and attitudes which so influence what people do as individuals and as a society, it is these ideas which must be changed so that they reflect more accurately the reality of poverty. Such a change could result in the emergence of a greater understanding of what is involved in people being people and what their search for fulfilment demands. Only then can the task begin of rebuilding a more accurate view of the poor which should lead into better beliefs about people and into better beliefs about God.

How the Poor are seen in Relation to the Rich: Perceptions and Attitudes about Equality.

Since the poor cannot be considered properly without reference to the affluent society in which they live, it is necessary to complete the picture by looking at what people feel about the relationship between rich and poor in Britain today.

Many now feel that they live in a far more equal society and that the gulf between rich and poor has been reduced significantly since the Second World War. That belief does not stand up to careful examination. The recent Royal Commission on the Distribution of Income and Wealth noted that despite a levelling process from 1939–48, the 50s and 60s saw a reversion to earlier inequalities. Rather than a picture of growing equality, they presented a view of 'short-run fluctuations in a more stable and continuing inequality'. The false perception of increasing equality is linked to a reluctance to recognize the persistence of serious class distinctions. The refusal to face up to the existence of grave social divisions is part and parcel of the general feeling that people are all now in the same class whether it be working class or middle class.

Inaccurate perceptions about growing equality are again reflected in the inaccurate reasons given for such a growth. These are connected with a belief in the reduction of the numbers of rich and poor. For example, at one end of the spectrum, there is an unsubstantiated belief that the rich have become relatively poorer through increased taxation (the myth of the overtaxed high salary earner). At the other end of the spectrum, there is the complementary belief that the poor either no longer exist, or if they do, they are certainly not suffering from the poverty of the 30s. The belief in a growing equalisation of income and wealth is also associated with the obvious and general increase in living standards. Yet increasing national wealth has not altered for the better the relationship between the bottom earners and the rest of society (the myth that growth removes poverty and produces greater equality).

23

The creation of the Welfare State, too, is seen by many as removing the need for poverty ('there's always the National Assistance'), and, indeed, as contributing to poverty by encouraging idleness. Yet the common assumption that a growing equality is directly associated with an over-generous expenditure of public funds on the Welfare State is once again not borne out by the facts. Even before the present cutbacks in public expenditure, Britain was proposing to spend less on its social services as a proportion of total production than were seven out of eight other Common Market states.

In each of these ways of looking at poverty it has been noted what so many people *actually* but wrongly feel about the poor and about equality. It is now possible to explore what are more accurate and adequate reasons why the poor should be taken seriously.

2. Why be Involved with the Poor, and What Happens as a Result.

It is easy for Christians to justify their involvement with the poor by reference to a Bible which talks of God siding with the poor and opposing the rich. Indeed in many Church circles it is now the current fashion to mention at every possible opportunity God's solidarity with the poor. Yet their talk often remains general and their responses accordingly unspecific. By avoiding facing up to poverty through the lives of people like Mary, Mike, Ann, Jim, Barbara, Dave and Mr and Mrs Brown they are unable to talk about God and the Church through the realities of poverty.

They are unable to do this because they do not begin from where people are in their understanding of poverty with all their false perceptions and attitudes. To begin with, this reality is important because only by challenging it in the light of what is now known about poverty can adequate reasons for involvement with the poor begin to emerge. The justification for sustaining involvement in the issue of poverty cannot arise out of a thoroughly defective understanding of what it is and what caused it. It can only emerge by facing up to and changing false perceptions and attitudes. The reasons for involvement will then be seen to be addressing important truths about human living and Christian belief. It will be seen that people should be involved with the poor because of what the poor tell them about themselves and about Christian belief and discipleship.

What the poor tell us about people rich and poor.
There are two major reasons why people should be concerned with the question of poverty in today's society. Both show how facing up to reality highlights important human concerns.

First, if people's perceptions of poverty are often inaccurate, then there is an obligation to find out what is really happening about poverty in society. There is a need to become familiar with the classic definitions of poverty (what it is) and with what these mean in terms of the numbers of poor in society (how many). It is important, too, to discover why there are still so many poor in today's affluent society. Good practices and policies can never flourish if the truth about an issue is neglected.

Secondly, if people's attitudes to the poor are also often wrong, what morally adequate attitudes should guide people's involvement with the poor? If an essential truth about poverty is that it is created by social forces outside the control of the poor, then compassion becomes an essential response to the predicament of the poor. Men and women need to be concerned with the poor because there is something about being human which drives people to care for others and especially for those less able to help themselves. What is common to the stories of Mary, Mike, Ann, Jim, Barbara, Dave, and Mr and Mrs Brown is that however hard they try there are grave and insuperable limits to what their self-help can achieve. Unless things are done by the more fortunate and by society as a whole to break the debilitating constraints of their poverty, there is little future for these four families and the millions like them. The question is not whether we should care for the poor. If people are of value in their own right and if to be human is to care, then compassion suggests no alternative. The only question facing the basic humanity of men and women is how they should care. It is by this criterion in particular that the moral credibility of individuals, societies, philosophies and theologies is judged. In the words of a great Christian layman, R.H. Tawney, there is 'no touchstone, except the treatment of childhood, which reveals the true character of a social philosophy more clearly than the spirit in which it regards the misfortunes of those of its members who fall by the way'.

Far more lies behind these classic reasons for involvement with the poor than first meets the eye. For example, everyone will be driven to take such caring seriously even if only for reasons of self-concern. The realities behind the creation and exacerbation of contemporary poverty increasingly influence everyone's quality of life. The disturbing decline of British manufacturing industry will influence inevitably society's ability to care adequately for the sick, the young and the elderly, and those without employment. This will affect the poor first and foremost, but then every other citizen. The decline also produces that large-scale and long-term unemployment which eats like a cancer into the lives of millions of individuals, their families and their communities. No one can now assume that they are immune from its threat, from the poverty which has so diminished the lives of Mike and Ann.

It behoves everyone too to take poverty seriously because of its contribution to grave social disruption as the summer riots of 1981 revealed. Mrs Thatcher's comment, at the 1980 Lord Mayor's Banquet, that 'Poverty, wherever it exists, is the enemy of stability' only confirms the importance of this justification for involvement in the poverty issue. Prudence as well as altruism requires everyone to take the caring imperative seriously.

To pay such careful attention to poverty will lead inevitably beyond the poor. It will mean examining affluence as well as poverty, and the social ordering of society as well as the experience of individuals. It drives people to see that the poor represent in their lives that fracturing of fellowship endemic in humanity but so characteristic in the plight of the poor. The reality of the divisions between 'them' and 'us', managers and workers, and council houses and private estates, is crystallized powerfully in the lives of the poor. Both within our four families and more especially in their separation from ordinary life, the whole quality of their relationships with each other and with the outside world is stultified. That which is necessary for people and their fulfilment as held out to men and women by God is significantly denied them.

The question of relationships between people lies, of course, at the centre of the debates over both poverty and equality. By equality is not meant making all the same, as though different personalities, needs and talents can be ignored. Nor does it refer to the legal right to a fair trial or the vote. Rather, equality should be seen as implying a situation in which social conditions enjoyed by all members of the State are not so vastly different that they make it impossible for certain members to enter into the advantages of normal living. Without this minimum and equitable access to resources, it clearly becomes imposs-ible to attain that promotion of each person's uniqueness 'without regard to the vulgar irrelevancies of class and income' which lies at the heart of equality. Freedom in relationships, which lies at the heart of love and therefore of what makes people people, is so threatened by poverty as to be often unachievable by the poor.

Facing up to the truth about poverty, when associated with caring for those less able to help themselves, not only provides powerful reasons for involvement in the issue of poverty. It thereby also points to that which is important about the humanity of all men and women in which all should share but in which many clearly do not. Involve-ment with poverty can therefore develop into involvement with the poor as a means of ensuring that all have the possibility of realistically seeking their fulfilment. To pursue this for all becomes an extension of the pursuit of this for oneself. A proper caring for others is always related to a proper caring for self. That is why the poor should be taken seriously.

What the Poor tell us about Christian Belief and Discipleship.

The invitation to be involved with the poor offers people the opportunity to face up to reality and to care for others. For Christians who accept this invitation there should also emerge a better understanding of Christian belief and discipleship.

First, to be involved with the poor challenges inaccurate understandings of the poor. By getting at the truth of the matter Christians are offered an opportunity to encounter the very nature of God. To become more aware of the genuine dimensions of the human predicament as revealed in the plight of the poor drives Christians to the centre of their belief. It enables them to be in a better position to understand the Christian story of God addressing the human predicament through Christ. It suggests an understanding of God as being concerned with the realities of life, where he can therefore be found, worshipped and served. It suggests that it is out of these realities that beliefs about and in God could emerge. It reflects a faith in a God who through Jesus Christ took upon himself the reality of our humanity and through this achieved our redemption. By seeking a better understanding of the human situation the Christian can find new ways of being open to God.

Yet the concern for what the poor and poverty are really about does not just drive one into a better understanding about both God's concern with humanity and the humanity of God. In so doing it also promotes a view of that humanity as it now is and to which all humans are now called, which also drives one to be concerned about poverty as a grave obstacle to that belief. If God both created people in his likeness and through that humanity

28

achieved salvation, then two beliefs about it can be seen to follow. First, if men and women are so valued by God then they should so value one another. If poverty means distress and disadvantage for some valued people and not for others, then it is plainly unacceptable. Secondly, having such a common source and end in God, men and women are now in a family relationship with one another. Those economic and social differences which serve to create divisions between people threaten to destroy the reality and possibility of such a fellowship.

Each of these beliefs about people appears to suggest a belief in a form of equality as 'the necessary corollary of the Christian conception of man'. They enshrine a concern for people as having far more in common than divides them, and therefore warranting their treatment as people of equal worth. They promote a community of relationships out of a deep sense that all are created by God and are part of the divine purpose. They drive one to oppose any infringement of human rights as an infringement of God's purposes and therefore an infringement of God himself.

In all these ways the Christian is concerned with what it means to be human because that is what God created, what God became, and therefore what in his Incarnation he is. To be concerned with humanity in the form of the poor is therefore a kind of taking part in God. Indeed, it is through a sensitivity to the human reality of the poor that God has always particularly worked to make known his demands for righteousness and his offer of salvation. The question so often asked in the Church about what is distinctively Christian about this understanding of such human reality is therefore very disturbing. It can suggest that Christianity demands something different from reality, and therefore neglects the great divine truth of God being encountered and served through the reality of an accurate understanding of the poor. Christianity makes a difference to these matters not by adding to reality, but in terms of what can be found in reality.

Secondly, to be concerned to get at the truth about

poverty does not simply offer a greater understanding of God. Such a concern also suggests a pattern of involvement in life which enables Christians to practise a pattern of discipleship which follows the divine involvement in society. As God through Christ took upon himself the realities of humanity to achieve redemption, so men and women can likewise take these realities upon themselves and through them participate in that process of redemption. Yet for Christians to be concerned with humanity in the form of the poor offers even more. A concern for the poor and under-privileged is also one of the great moral imperatives emerging out of the Judaeo-Christian tradition. It is as though concern for the poor is one of the great tests of whether people really are concerned for the human.

Involvement with the poor provides Christians with more than an understanding of God and the opportunity to practise a more faithful discipleship. It also suggests what the Church should be like as the fellowship of such believers and practisers. When tested by that calling the Church has often been found wanting. Indeed, the failure of the British Church to take seriously the truth about poverty especially as it affects the unskilled working classes may be one of the greatest indictments which can be brought against it.

Conclusion

Taking the poor seriously offers to all both the opportunity to be fully human and also freedom from that destructive concern so often associated with the so-called distinctively Christian. It does so by showing how that concern cannot properly be separated from a pursuit of what it means to be fully human. Indeed, it does far more, in that through this it also powerfully contributes to an understanding of God and the practise of discipleship. And since that pursuit is so seriously challenged by the realities of poverty, there is no other course but to be involved with the poor. That is why the poor must be taken seriously.

PART TWO

The Reality of Poverty:
What Analysis Reveals and Suggests

CHAPTER THREE
What is Poverty?

In discussions about the nature of poverty, people grudgingly accept the evidence of widespread belief that 'real poverty' no longer exists and that even if it does then 'it's the poor's own fault'. Despite the upset caused by these revelations (because so many share these false perceptions and attitudes), many are sufficiently aware that all is not well in society and that arguments about poverty have something to do with the present malaise. Yet people then rightly demand more knowledge about this thing called poverty before they agree to take it seriously.

Of course none of this disbelief and unease is new. In the 1870s and then in the 1950s many felt that poverty was no longer a serious social problem. It took the work of Charles Booth and Seebohm Rowntree at the turn of the century, and Peter Townsend and Brian Abel-Smith in the 1950s to correct these false perceptions and attitudes about poverty. There was also a recognition over a century ago, that questions about poverty lay at the root of many of Britain's problems. In 1869 the radical MP Bright declared in the House of Commons, 'Why is there so much poverty in this country? This is the great problem in comparison with which many of these piddling questions which sometimes occupy us are nothing'. Given this historical perspective we are faced with the fact that whatever contemporary poverty is, it has continued to be part of our kind of industrial society from its beginnings until the present. We have to come to terms with the question of the persistence as well as the existence of poverty.

Against this background, to discover the nature and extent of poverty in contemporary Britain involves a search for a definition of poverty and then estimating how much of it there is; it means recognizing who the poor are and what their poverty means for them; and since poverty exists in an affluent society, what, if any, is the connection between poverty and inequality?

1. WHAT IS POVERTY? DEFINITIONS AND EXTENT.

A WORD FOR IT

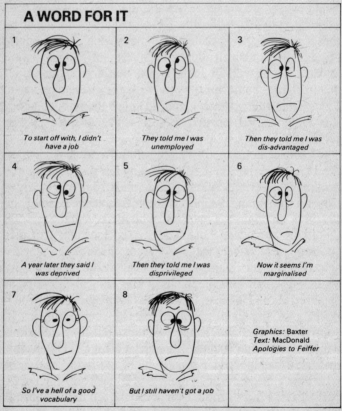

1. To start off with, I didn't have a job

2. They told me I was unemployed

3. Then they told me I was dis-advantaged

4. A year later they said I was deprived

5. Then they told me I was disprivileged

6. Now it seems I'm marginalised

7. So I've a hell of a good vocabulary

8. But I still haven't got a job

Graphics: Baxter
Text: MacDonald
Apologies to Feiffer

However well you try to define poverty you will get it wrong in someone's view. Any survey of the nature and extent of poverty will be selective. It will represent as much an interpretation of a complex reality as a statement of fact. Not surprisingly therefore there are widely differing and constantly changing views as to what poverty is: witness the plight of our hero above. Given the arguments over terminology, his confusion as to what he is in the eyes of society and the experts is understandable. Yet he is not confused over the one matter of real importance: he has not got a job; he is poor, as the families in our case studies are poor. It is this basic clarity over what is really important which constitutes a grave warning to all who use differences of view over the nature of poverty as a means of not taking it seriously. It is a warning which applies equally to those who build up a great knowledge about poverty and then do precious little about it. When R.H. Tawney surveyed the vast number of reports about the nature and persistence of poverty throughout this century, he concluded that the building of a more just society, like the Kingdom of Heaven, 'cometh not by observation'!

There are two main definitions of poverty to consider. The first major one relates to a bare subsistence level and the second to an understanding of the essentially relative nature of poverty. Both are important because they lead to different estimates of the numbers in poverty. Both should be considered only in the light of the previous warnings, and each needs to be reformulated.

(a) *Subsistence Poverty* is the State's definition of a poverty line and is related to the supplementary benefit level of income and to the standard of living it allows. It includes all who receive supplementary benefit or who receive incomes equivalent to it or below it. Based on a limited definition of needs, it inevitably reflects a narrow concept of income and is concerned to maintain the physical efficiency of people. Although it allows for only a severely restricted way of life, it is above the starvation level.

In order to understand fully the subsistence definition of poverty, it is necessary to see how it arose. From the sixteenth through to the nineteenth century, there was a concern in society to find ways of guaranteeing a minimum sustenance to all its members. Despite these efforts, the work of Charles Booth and Seebohm Rowntree at the end of the nineteenth century revealed with great precision the disturbing nature of a poverty which had mushroomed with the growth of industrial and urban life. To quantify the amount of such poverty both had to produce operational definitions. For Booth, writing in 1889, the 'poor' were 'those whose means may be sufficient, but are barely sufficient, for decent independent life'. The 'very poor' were 'those whose means are insufficient for this according to the usual standard of life in this country'. Some twelve years later, Seebohm Rowntree recognized that many of the poor were in reality very poor because of the normal misfortunes of life like sickness, old age or unemployment. Poverty was therefore about families whose 'total earnings are insufficient to obtain the minimum necessaries for the maintenance of merely physical efficiency'. It was from this definition that Rowntree worked out and costed the minimum diet, clothing and shelter necessary to keep the labourer alive and at work. A generation later, Beveridge based National Assistance payments on these principles which now form the basis of the supplementary benefit system.

These benefit levels as a proportion of the average earnings in a society have remained essentially unaltered despite some other more obvious changes. Changes for the better there undoubtedly have been, when today's standards are compared with the 1930s. Present supplementary benefit levels are 25 per cent better than the minimum requirements for physical efficiency determined by Rowntree in the 1930s. From 1948 to 1979, too, benefits have increased by more than double the increase in the Retail Price Index. Yet, as a percentage of average earnings, benefits have remained pretty constant. For example, a married couple with two children drew a benefit of 39 per cent of gross average earnings in 1948. By 1979, this had only risen to 41.6 per cent. When compared to the living standards of the rest of society, the essential relationship between social security benefits and the kind of living they allow has therefore remained virtually unaltered for generations.

In beginning to build up a definition of subsistence poverty in terms of the supplementary benefit level, there is an important question as to whether the supplementary benefit level can be regarded as equivalent to being in poverty. The aim of the supplementary benefit is ostensibly to cover all the claimants' normal needs. It assumes that 'To keep out of poverty, they must have an income which enables them to participate in the life of the community. They must be able, for example, to keep themselves reasonably well fed, and well enough dressed to maintain their self-respect and to attend interviews for jobs with confidence. Their homes must be reasonably warm; their children should not feel ashamed by the quality of their clothing; their family must be able to visit relatives, and give them something on their birthdays and at Christmas time; they must be able to read newspapers and retain their television sets and their membership of trade unions and churches'.

The reality is quite different. As the accounts of our families revealed, the theoretical aim of supplementary benefit is not realised in practice. Even with careful budgetting, the way of life on supplementary benefit offers only a bleak existence. Why is there such a gulf between intention and actuality? Why is it that the supplementary level can be taken as a *measurement* of poverty when in theory it is supposed to *protect* people from it?

The answer lies, as already noted, in the history of the definition of poverty. When Rowntree worked out what was the minimum necessary to keep the labourer's body and soul together, he assumed a diet worse than the workhouse's, and a frugality which was not only beyond the reach of ordinary people but which even then allowed for no emergencies. Yet it was on this understanding with some allowance made for changing patterns of life, that Beveridge based his National Assistance scheme. But even this is not quite true, because in certain important respects Beveridge pitched his benefit levels below even those of Rowntree. In particular, he gravely underestimated the needs of children.

It was this defective legacy which helped to ensure that the existing supplementary benefit scheme provides a poverty line rather than the escape from poverty which was originally intended. Indeed, the Welfare State as it now operates is so implicated in the creation and maintenance of poverty that it must be regarded as a major cause of deprivation. A number of government and other surveys support this conclusion. A survey in 1972 into whether the sick and unemployed on benefits have sufficient clothing, revealed that 61 per cent of the sick and disabled with families had less than the supplementary benefit's suggested minimum stock. 76 per cent of the unemployed with families fell below this acceptable level. Both groups were in serious debt for food, clothing, heating and housing. Another survey in 1975 showed how the allowances for children were 'totally inadequate to provide enough food, even if 75 per cent of the benefit was spent on food in the most efficient manner'.

Confirmation of this evidence that supplementary benefit levels ensure for most a life in poverty can be found in the additional payments made to enable people to buy clothes and shoes. If there were 292,000 such payments made in 1979, then clearly supplementary benefit was inadequate to meet everyday needs. It did not keep people out of poverty, and since 1979, the position has taken a serious turn for the worse. In the last two years, as unemployment doubled and trebled, social security benefits for the unemployed were cut. Benefits in general, originally too low and therefore almost ensuring the poverty of clients, have also been deliberately reduced in relation to inflation. The poor are being driven into greater poverty by the very system which Beveridge designed as a net below which people could not fall. The net now also ensures they do not rise.

So strong is the connection between poverty and the level of income associated with supplementary benefit that most commentators including the DHSS now define poverty as those with incomes up to either 20 per cent or 40 per cent above the supplementary benefit level. This enlargement of the subsistence definition of poverty is also justified because the State in practice observes a higher standard than the basic benefit rates by disregarding certain minor amounts of claimants' incomes and by adding, for certain claimants, small amounts to the basic benefits.

The extent of subsistence poverty. On the basis of this definition of poverty (as of all those below, at, or marginally above the supplementary benefit line), how many people are poor? What are the statistics of poverty? At the mention of statistics many people switch off. They either seize up at the first sight of figures, or, more likely, criticize some of the figures as a means of rejecting the existence of poverty on any large scale. Yet for those concerned to get at the truth about poverty there is no alternative but to move, in the words of Charles Booth, from 'the emotional superstructure' to 'the statistical base'. For him, poverty was not simply about individual men and women, but about what happens to certain types of people in certain situations. To understand the sheer nature and extent of such a problem always involves quantifying those social forces which shape and manifest themselves in people. To treat people with the attention they deserve requires not only taking seriously the faces of individual persons, but also the facts behind their faces. It means that when looking into an old man's face, one sees through the beauty of a unique being into the fact that he is one of nine-and-a-half million retired people and very vulnerable to poverty. To make sense of that total reality demands engaging his face and all the facts it contains. It requires making sense of statistics. It means that those who reject statistics do not really care about people and their problems. They belong rather to the world of false perceptions and attitudes.

The numbers in subsistence poverty can be seen in the following table.

	1975	1977	1979
Below Supp. Benefit (SB).	1,840,000	2,020,000	2,100,000
Receiving SB.	3,710,000	4,120,000	3,980,000
Total	5,550,000	6,140,000	6,080,000

When those up to *10 per cent* above

SB added:	6,670,000	7,470,000	7,150,000
Up to *20 per cent* above SB:	8,300,000	9,530,000	8,620,000
Up to *40 per cent* above SB:	12,540,000	13,110,000	11,290,000

NB: 1. The definition of poverty as up to 10 per cent, 20 per cent or 40 per cent above supplementary benefit level has been discussed above.

2. Since 1979, the numbers on supplementary benefit (and in the other categories) have increased sharply. There are now thought to be about six million people dependent on it.

3. Because the Government has changed the way in which it calculates the number of people at different income levels, it is not strictly legitimate to compare the figures for 1975, with those for 1977 and 1979.

(Source: Department of Health and Social Security, *Low Income Families*, 1979.)

(b)   *Poverty as Relative Deprivation*. There is a growing unease with the subsistence definition of poverty. Many regard it as inaccurate and ungenerous with regard to what is needed even for physical subsistence. An even more damaging criticism is the awareness that poverty is about far more than a family's lack of finance. It concerns their whole way of life as part of a local community in a wider society in a particular period of history. A narrow view of poverty concentrated on an individual's subsistence fails to recognize adequately that people live in communities as social beings with needs and spending habits shaped by local conventions and nationally approved standards.

In the light of such criticisms there has developed a search for a definition of poverty which acknowledges changes in the patterns of living and recognizes the isolation from the normal operations of society which poverty so often entails. With regard to the former, the need is clearly great. Whether in housing, where 1,244,000 dwellings were considered to be unfit for human habitation in 1971, or in employment, where one in two could be without work in inner urban areas in 1981, there is 'a failure to attain certain social norms to which existing social policies are apparently intended to provide access'. In each of these great sectors of life and in many others including education, health and in rural situations transport, many in our society lack proper access to services or live in situations without basic amenities. They are deprived of what most people in Britain take for granted. It is because of this lack of access to the resources for normal living that the poor are marginalised in our society. Their inability to choose to pursue normal patterns of life produces their profound sense of isolation from so much of what goes on around them. It means that 'you can't enjoy life like everyone else'. Watching Christmas adverts for toys on commercial television with prices ranging from £10 to over £100 must only confirm the alienation of millions of families and children totally dependent on State benefits. They must feel totally shut out of society and cut off from normal life.

A definition of poverty as relative deprivation therefore highlights the lack of resources necessary to allow a person or family to participate 'in the activities, customs and diets commonly approved by society...' Their resources of income, housing, education, and health are 'so seriously below those commanded by the average individual or family that they are, in effect, excluded from ordinary living patterns, customs and activities'. As an Under Secretary of State at the DHSS has noted, 'It is not sufficient to assess poverty by absolute standards: nowadays, it must be judged on relative criteria by comparison with the standard of living of other groups in the community'.

The extent of poverty as relative deprivation is very difficult to estimate since it concerns the more 'subjective' area of styles of living. Peter Townsend has managed to calculate the number of people in relative deprivation as approximately 12,460,000.

Concluding Note on the Two Definitions. To play off the two definitions of subsistence poverty and relative deprivation against each other is both inaccurate and unprofitable. It is inaccurate because it neglects the past and present awareness of a relative dimension within the subsistence definition of poverty. Both Booth and Rowntree understood that 'the standard of living of the poor was not absolute but related to the general living standards of the community'. And this concern has always been part of supplementary benefit policy through its allowances for changes in consumer patterns like provision for the standard TV license. It is inaccurate too, because it is clear that the long-term unemployed experience poverty both in itself, in terms of the meagre standard of living afforded by basic supplementary benefit rates, and in relation to what many of them earned when in employment.

To argue the case of one definition against the other is also unprofitable. It communicates to the public a lack of certainty which confirms their existing reluctance to take poverty seriously. It benefits no-one and least of all the poor.

In the light of these observations one is therefore driven to a definition of poverty which includes both subsistence and relativity. It means that poverty becomes: *the burden of being on a low income and being without access to many of the things associated with living normal ordinary lives in today's society*.

2. Characteristics of Poverty.

In the light of the experience of our four families and of our emerging definition of poverty, what are the main features of poverty as it affects the lives of people, and as it affects the groups which are most vulnerable to poverty?

(a) Poverty As It Affects People.

Whether one considers the extremes of poverty as found in many large families or whether one detects the poverty hidden below the surface of the apparent normality of many lives, it is the same reality which is affecting different people. These patterns of life shape the existence of millions in terms of (i) their life style, and (ii) their relationships.

(i) *Poverty as it restricts the life style of people (the reality of subsistence poverty)*. Perhaps the most daunting effect of poverty concerns the numerous and conflicting demands made on the family's unmanageably limited budget. Years of struggling to make ends meet results in people having no material, emotional or social reserves left to meet the inevitable emergencies of life. Their vulnerable, precarious position can be likened to a man 'standing permanently up to the neck in water, so that even a ripple is sufficient to drown him'. The drowning takes the form of being driven into debt. Living in poor, ill-heated and often rented accommodation only exacerbates their predicament. It is not surprising, therefore, that stressful living in poor environments produces poor health. The human cost of poverty can be seen in the faces and figures of the prematurely aged, in the 40-year-olds being mistaken for the retired. As the Chairman of the Supplementary Benefits Commission observed, 'anyone meeting families who live on supplementary benefits, and walking through the streets where they abound, constantly sees pinched and pallid faces and shoulders hunched against the wind under shoddy plastic clothing'.

All these problems are made so much worse 'by the sheer drudgery and monotony of such restricted standards of living'. It is as though the poor are so enslaved by their predicament as to be unable to make effective choices now or to plan ahead. Perhaps the most disturbing aspect of poverty is that it rarely stimulates people to change their lot. Indeed, so often it makes it more unlikely.

(ii) *Poverty as it restricts the relationships of people (the reality of relative deprivation)*. Poverty can never be properly considered only in terms of its impact on the life of an individual or family. It always profoundly affects the life of a person within the community both in one's self-understanding and in one's relationships with others. On the one hand it has a most damaging effect on the quality of family life in the form of divorces, suicides, abortions, children in care, delinquencies, violence and accidents. Not that more affluent families do not experience similar problems. They obviously do, but because of their access to finance, and good education, health and housing they do not become public problems. On the other hand, as noted already, poverty powerfully affects the relationships of the poor with their neighbours and the wider society through inaccurate perceptions and false attitudes. The stigma of poverty is not a deterrent which prevents poverty. It only doubles the burden of deprivation for the poor and for society. It only ensures that the poor both feel and are made to feel marginal to the mainstream life of society. It is this sense and reality of powerlessness which robs their citizenship of so much of its value. Surely such poverty is doubly offensive to any real sense of humanity or justice?

(b)   Poverty As It Affects Groups.

Of course many people and families experience poverty at some stage of their life, whether it be when the children first arrive or when retirement is reached. Yet many never actually escape out of the poverty trap once they are in it. Some such people and therefore groups have always been more vulnerable to poverty than others. It was eighty years ago that Rowntree noted that the elderly and young families were particularly susceptible to poverty. That observation is still relevant today as a survey of the groups of people particularly vulnerable to poverty will reveal.

The elderly. Many people become poor as soon as they pass retirement age. This is revealed by the fact that out of nine and a half million elderly people, over two million have to depend on supplementary benefit in addition to their pensions (in 1978, 44 per cent of those on supplementary benefit were retired). Even then, over 800,000 lived below this poverty line (unclaimed benefits by the elderly totalled over £60 million per annum). All this poverty exists despite Beveridge's plan that by 1956 everyone would receive an adequate pension. It is important to note that the poverty of the elderly includes a vulnerability to ill-health and a likelihood of poor housing in addition to income deprivation.

Single women and aged dependents. To give up a job in order to care for an aged parent almost inevitably results in a drop in income and increased social costs. Like the low-paid, this group does not appear in supplementary benefit statistics even though there could be 300,000 such people.

One-parent families. Marriage breakdown (which is an increasing reality), or the death of a spouse mean that there are at least 850,000 single parents with at least one and a half million children. They are a particularly fast-growing group (a 32 per cent increase from 1971–6) and are very vulnerable to poverty, with nearly 50 per cent being dependent on supplementary benefit (339,000 in 1978). There are about 40,000 such families with 70,000 children living below this poverty line. Theirs is a poverty compounded by poor housing and can result in children under-achieving at school.

Families in general. In 1977, 33 per cent of families (7,640,000) were living below, on, or up to 40 per cent above the supplementary benefit line. Of the 14,020,000 people involved, 3,570,000 were children (38.1 per cent of all children). According to a government survey, if women at work stopped at home to look after their children and release jobs for their menfolk, then the number of families living on about the poverty line would rise to about 15,640,000 (61.2 per cent).

Children. It has been noted already how many children are affected by poverty. A survey of all children born between the 3rd and the 9th March 1958, and checked in 1969, confirmed these sad facts. It showed that more than one child in every three (36 per cent) was in either a one-parent family or a large family, a low-income family, or badly housed, and that one in every sixteen was affected by each of these three indices of family composition, low income and poor housing.

The sick and disabled. Sickness is a major cause of poverty which affects especially unskilled and semi-skilled manual worker families. They have more days off than other social classes and yet have the worst sick-pay schemes. (The unskilled are three times more vulnerable to chronic sickness than professional workers). In 1975, 255,000 sick and disabled people were receiving supplementary benefit. Over 570,000 sick and disabled and their dependants were living below 120 per cent of supplementary benefit rates.

The low-paid. It is a sad commentary on a society applauding the virtues of work that there were over 3.3 million low paid workers who actually earned their poverty including 640,000 living below the State poverty line. (By low-paid is meant those earning less than two thirds of the average wage. The 1979 figures include 2.5 million women and 0.8 million men, plus their dependants. If part-time workers were also included, a further 1.7 million women and 126,000 men would be added). Of course, this understanding of poverty does not even begin to ask 'how many people are in worthwhile rather than dead-end or socially useless jobs', with poor working conditions, lower pensions and sick-pay, and a greater vulnerability to unemployment, (manual workers are three times more likely than non-manual workers to become unemployed).

The unemployed. The relentless growth of large-scale unemployment to over three million has been accompanied by an equally disturbing rise in the number of long-term unemployed to over one million in 1982. It is this latter group which is totally dependent on supplementary benefit and who are therefore most likely to experience harsh poverty.

There are a number of common strands which link these different experiences of poverty, and the most disturbing and powerful is social class. It is always the unskilled manual worker and his family who bear the disproportionate burden of low incomes, low pay, unemployment, poor housing, bad health, and defective education. Nearly 50 per cent of the unskilled live below, at, or on the margins of the State poverty line. Even in death these inequalities persist. If unskilled men and women aged 15–64 had experienced the same chances of death as professional people during the years 1959–63, 40,000 would not have died.

Faced with the cumulative evidence of poverty as essentially a class phenomenon, there appears to be no way of avoiding the sad but disturbing conclusion that our society condones the existence of a substantial underclass of citizens. It is not simply that those living off unearned State benefits, the sick, the disabled, the children, the unemployed and the elderly are thereby condemned to a 'miserable way of life'. It is also that even those with access to more resources through earned income include a sizeable minority of nearly 20 per cent of wage-earners who are paid only at about the State poverty line. To put such benefit and wage recipients together produces an underclass in relation to the standard of living enjoyed by the majority of the population.

3. Poverty as Inequality.

Why is it necessary to look at inequality in a discussion about poverty? The answer lies at the heart of the understanding of poverty. If the definition of poverty includes a recognition that it is about not being able to do what others do, then we are clearly pushed into the area of the social divisions in society. The recognition that poverty and riches are the two sides of the same coin is part of a long tradition stretching from the Old Testament prophets to Townsend in the 1980s. It is a tradition represented by the advice of R.H. Tawney who recommended the student of poverty 'to start much higher up the stream than the point he wishes to reach; that what thoughtful rich people call the problem of poverty, thoughtful poor people call with equal justice the problem of riches'.

Problems associated with defining poverty as inequality.
There are two particular issues raised by any linking of poverty and inequality. First, talking of poverty only in terms of the position of the poor relative to others is open to serious questioning. Conditions have improved over the years for everyone, and there will presumably always be some people poorer than others. All members of our society have benefitted from increased standards of living. These do not necessarily benefit the poor by reducing the gap between them and the rest, but the poor do get better off, they do have their TVs and many do have telephones and cars. Similarly, but on an international level, the bottom 20 per cent in Sweden are poor in Swedish terms but significantly richer than the bottom 20 per cent in the USA. Inequality should never simply be equated with poverty.

Secondly, to sustain the idea of poverty as inequality means that the 'relativity' understanding of poverty as a way into the issue of inequality must always be supplemented by the 'subsistence' understanding of poverty. General labourers in the North West suffer grave inequality in relation to other occupational groupings because of their vastly greater vulnerability to unemployment. In November 1981, there were 22,601 registered unemployed professional and managerial workers competing for 1,421 vacancies (a ratio of 16:1). At the same time and in the same region there were 123,642 unemployed general labourers competing for 181 vacancies (a ratio of 679:1). Yet general labourers are also poor because their vulnerability can be measured in terms of the income many of them received from supplementary benefit (the long-term unemployed received an average of £25.79 per week supplementary benefit in 1979). Therefore the damaging significance of poverty as inequality is not just that some have less opportunities and resources than others. It is that that less is unable to sustain people in a normal and reasonable life.

The nature and extent of inequality. The accuracy of the generally held perception of growing equality of income and wealth in our society has already been questioned. This exposure of the myth of equality becomes complete when the devastating facts of inequality are considered.

According to the Royal Commission on the Distribution of Income and Wealth, the estimated total value of personal wealth in 1973 was £163 thousand million. The top 10 per cent of the population in 1975, aged eighteen and over, owned 60 per cent of this wealth, whereas the bottom 80 per cent owned only 23.8 per cent. The ownership of wealth in the form of shares, government bonds and financial deposits, is even more unevenly distributed, with the top 1 per cent owning over 80 per cent of *privately* held stocks and shares. (Most stocks and shares are held by insurance and pension funds).

Despite a limited redistribution of wealth (essentially from the very rich to the rich), all the underlying trends suggest 'the continuing high concentration of wealth in Britain compared with other countries'. For example, in the USA the proportion of total wealth owned by the top 1 per cent is only half as large as that held by the top 1 per cent in Britain. In Malcolm Dean's ironic words: 'The only thing which is equal about the distribution of our wealth is its symmetry: the top fifth owning four fifths of the nation's wealth, and the bottom four fifths a mere fifth'.

The picture of income distribution reveals a similar picture of great inequality remaining virtually unchanged for generations. The bottom 50 per cent received 24.1 per cent of all incomes in 1976–7 (compared to 23.7 per cent in 1949), whereas the top 10 per cent received 26.2 per cent in 1976–7 (compared to 33.2 per cent in 1949). The better-off have therefore not been losing ground as governments would have us believe. Instead, since the mid-1970s higher income groups have been steadily increasing their share of the nation's total personal income.

Perhaps most disturbing of all is the fact that the earnings of the bottom 10 per cent of adult male manual workers have remained at 68 per cent of average earnings from 1886 to 1980. (The top 10 per cent earned 49 per cent more than the average compared with 43 per cent in 1886!) When to these inequalities is added what life is like for the bottom 10 per cent in terms of bad health, poor housing, dramatic underrepresentation in higher education (only Portugal and Ireland in Western Europe have a worse record for working-class children staying on at school), poor wages and conditions, and a high risk of unemployment, then there is only one conclusion to be drawn. Any adequate understanding of poverty must include more than an understanding of poverty as the threat of bare subsistence, as 'hearing the babies cry because they are hungry or cold'. Nor is it enough to add an understanding of poverty as relative deprivation, as 'when you can't enjoy life like everyone else'. It must also include the recognition that poverty is a principal expression of the profound inequalities which lie at the heart of British society. All these aspects of poverty need to be understood and held together in the definition of poverty.

CHAPTER FOUR
Why is there Poverty?

Nearly eighty years ago Edward Caird, the great Master of Balliol, urged Beveridge and Tawney to go to the East End 'to discover why with so much wealth, there was also so much poverty in London'. As a result of taking Caird's advice, Beveridge became the author of the modern Welfare State, and Tawney became a great economic historian, adult educationalist and social moralist. Yet despite their heroic efforts, they and many others have been unable to remove the blight of severe deprivation from our society. The question, 'Why is there so much poverty in this country?' is still being heard 113 years after Bright first asked it in Parliament and forty years after the introduction of Beveridge and Tawney's Welfare State.

Why is it important to discover the reasons for the existence of poverty? The challenge of poverty is not simply or primarily associated with its weakening effect on the social cohesion of contemporary society. Its persistence over generations has an important effect on the moral credibility of a nation. It has disruptive implications for the practice of caring politics and religion. Throughout the long history of industrialization in Britain, the issue of poverty and its treatment has cast its shadow over governments in general and over the lives of politicians and churchmen in particular. In the face of these realities the existence of poverty demands more than description. It surely demands explanation. Careful definitions need to be complemented by careful investigations into what lies behind the problem of poverty.

Of course many see the search for more accurate definitions and explanations as distractions from that practical effort which is what is really needed to sort out problems like poverty. Many people hunger and thirst for 'no nonsense' practical proposals rather than theoretical discussions. They are the pragmatist's version of Tawney's more sophisticated judgment on the great mounds of 'poverty material'. He almost despairingly commented that 'what prevents effective action is, in the main, neither ignorance nor lack of resources but the absence of political will'. Yet there is nothing more impractical than those so-called practical people who take short-cuts to action by avoiding the hard preliminary work of analysis. How a problem is defined and then explained powerfully affects what is actually done about it. Whether people are conscious of this connection is neither here nor there. It is almost a matter of saying 'show us your suggestions for action and it will be possible to see what are your definitions and explanations'. Inaccurate perceptions of and defective attitudes to poverty invariably result in bad policies and practices. This is one of the major reasons why the question of poverty has persisted for generations. This is why it is necessary to explain what lies behind the reality of poverty.

There is a formula which can help people to get the truth behind poverty. It suggests a way of involvement in society which *analyses* a problem by defining it (including quantifying it) and then by explaining it. The *policies* or *practices* then promoted should be the implications of this analysis. It is this connection between *analysis* (as definition and explanation) and *practice* which lies at the heart of this study of poverty, (and which is equally useful for facing up to many other issues in our society). It should not be surprising therefore that each of the three main explanations of poverty to be examined in this chapter is associated with a particular view of the way society should be ordered. That connection will become even more evident when the three main ways of tackling the problem of poverty are discussed in Chapter Five. Their particular implications for Church policies will then be explored in Chapter Seven.

To explain the presence of poverty is not so much to identify its causes as to give an account of some of the factors which underlie its existence. There are three explanations of poverty which need to be examined. First, the explanation associated with the problems of individuals; secondly, the explanation associated with the problems of a community or area; and thirdly, the explanation associated with the class structure and institutional life of society.

1. THE INDIVIDUAL EXPLANATION OF POVERTY.

There are three main ways in which poverty is explained by reference to the problems of individuals. The first and most obvious popular explanation blames the victim. The second and third are less obvious but equally powerful and are associated with social work and politics.

(a) Many people in Britain believe that poverty is a self-inflicted wound. Such people see poverty as caused by a mixture of 'ill-luck, indolence and mismanagement'. They assume that individuals are wholly self-determining beings able to control their own destinies. Poverty is therefore attributed to individual failure, particularly since the creation of the Welfare State is supposed to allow all normal people to avoid poverty.

There are two other ways which do not blame the individual for his poverty but see it stemming from his limitations, deficiencies and maladjustments.

(b) There is a view of poverty, current in social-work-type experience, which sees it linked to the weaknesses of particular individuals and families rather than to the wider systems of society. In A.H. Halsey's words, it is a view which insists that 'the poor are different not primarily because of low income but because they have been habituated to poverty, and have developed a sub-culture of values adapted to these conditions which they pass on

53

to their children'. This understanding of the causes of poverty has two main expressions. On the one hand, there is the *cycle of deprivation* argument which sees the root cause of poverty in an individual or family's inability to deal with the normal tasks of living rather than its lack of money. Poor relationships in childhood are seen as producing inadequate personalities leading to early marriage, child neglect and an inability to manage money. Their children suffer from the same deprivations which are then repeated in their children. And so the cycle of deprivation is established and perpetuated.

On the other hand, there is the *culture of poverty* argument which traces the main cause of poverty to a way of life different from that of the surrounding society. Its chief contentions are that the poor are not integrated into major institutions like government bodies, education, and the churches; that there is a minimum of organization beyond the nuclear and extended family; that the sexual practices of the poor are at variance with the rest of society; and that their attitudes are ones of helplessness, dependency, inferiority, and little ability to defer gratification and to plan for the future. As poverty, such a 'culture' is transmitted to the next generation, (as with the cycle of deprivation) through child-rearing patterns. As a study in the USA suggested, the children of such a culture are 'trained only to repeat the failure, delinquency, crime and immoralities of those nearest them'.

(c) Lastly, there is an understanding of the political and economic functioning of society which assumes that society is made up of the sum total of individuals within it. The general welfare is served by individuals freely pursuing their self-interest in competition with others. Given the laws of supply and demand which operate in such a free market system, a person's income accordingly reflects his or her economic worth.

Since people are responsible for their actions and conditions, monetary rewards go to those with talent and effort. Poverty, according to Milton Friedman, has correspondingly to be attributed to the failings of the individual. 'Indigence was simply the punishment meted out to the improvident by their own lack of industry and efficiency. Far from being a blessed state, poverty was the obvious consequence of sloth and sinfulness'. Such a view of life not only seeks to enlarge the role of the individual by giving him more freedom and responsibility. It also seeks to reduce the role of the State especially in the fields of taxation and the Welfare State. Both, in the eyes of Rhodes Boyson, have contributed in recent years to the growth of poverty by taking money 'from the energetic, successful and thrifty to give to the idle, the failures and the feckless'. The all-providing State has resulted in the non-providing individual and family.

The three main ways of explaining poverty by reference to individuals are convincing to many. Yet they have obvious weaknesses when examined against the realities of poverty. First, they overlook and underestimate the *powerlessness* of the individual in a complex urban-industrial society. With 123,642 unemployed labourers chasing just 181 vacancies in the North West, and with nearly 40 per cent of the elderly living at about the State's poverty line, we are faced with something far more than the self-inflicted wounds of individuals. Even by 1890, the poverty of the unemployed was understood as being as much 'beyond their power to avert as if (it) had been natural calamities of fire, blood, or storm . . .'

Secondly, arguments from individualism clearly ignore the grossly unequal distribution of income, wealth and other resources like education, housing and health. So great are the disparities in these fields that they make any theoretical belief in equal opportunities for individuals virtually unworkable. Of course, everyone knows (and is constantly reminded of) the individual who drags himself out of poverty by his bootstraps. Tawney called such generalizing from the exception 'the tadpole philosophy'. Just because 100 tadpoles manage to get out of the pond and become frogs does not mean that all tadpoles can become frogs. The success of the 100 overlooks the destruction of the 10 million by ducks and little boys.

Thirdly, the virtues of hard-work, thrift and self-help are relevant only to people living well above the State poverty line. As Mr Heseltine has recently and correctly observed with regard to Liverpool 8, to talk of self-help in such situations is inappropriate. What do you help yourself with if you have no money, bad housing, poor health, virtually no education, and no hope of a job?

Fourthly, the view that the poor in their lives and culture are somehow different from the rest of society contradicts the research which suggests that in attitudes to work, education, sex, and language, the poor are not really so different. What the poor lack are the resources to live normal ordinary lives. They are in no way innately or qualitatively different from the rest of society.

2. THE AREA EXPLANATION OF POVERTY.

The second main explanation of poverty follows on closely from the first. It attributes the cause of poverty to the problems of communities rather than individuals. Poverty becomes a problem because of the imbalanced concentration of large numbers of poor people in particular areas. Problem individuals and families are grossed up into problem communities.

There is no doubt that this is an extremely attractive explanation of poverty. Indeed, so powerful is it that it has increasingly influenced the policies of successive governments. Beginning with the establishment of Educational Priority Areas in 1967–8, the Community Development Programme in 1969–70, Housing Action Areas and General Improvement Areas in 1974, and ending with the introduction of Enterprise Zones in 1980, governments have assumed that discrimination in favour of hard-hit areas will significantly erode the different forms of poverty.

Yet, as one walks the streets of a deprived area in inner city Salford, drinks in its pubs, works in its school and meets its people, one becomes increasingly clear that its predicament cannot simply be explained by reference to what goes on within it. There are two main reasons why this is so. First, poverty cannot be restricted to a particular area. For example, schools in Educational Priority Areas contain only two out of every five children recognized as disadvantaged. Further, within these EPA schools themselves, the majority of children are not disadvantaged. In more general terms too, the designation of poor areas always neglects the wide dispersion of poverty, especially as it affects rural as well as urban areas. Unless nearly half the country is included in the definition of deprived areas, there will always be more poor people living outside them than in.

Secondly, areas cannot be treated as autonomous or self-sufficient communities in terms of their economies and cultures. Their functioning and the allocation of resources to them are decided externally on a national basis. Decisions about employment, health, education and housing are invariably made elsewhere, and the more affluent areas nearly always gain most from such decision-making. Like the relationship of Third World to rich countries, the relative poverty of British regions and areas outside the South East can be fairly said to be a function of the richer region's prosperity. If economics are about the allocation of finite scarce resources, then if some areas have a greater share of them others will inevitably receive a smaller share. To limit an explanation of poverty to poor areas is to examine only one side of the equation. The answers will always be quite insufficient. Townsend noted that 'an area strategy cannot be the cardinal means of dealing with poverty'. It cannot be so because it is built upon an inaccurate area explanation of poverty.

3. THE CLASS AND INSTITUTIONAL EXPLANATION OF POVERTY.

To restrict the causes of poverty to individuals and areas is clearly an inadequate explanation of poverty. Even in 1912, Tawney noted how 'there is a unity underlying the individual cases of poverty; . . . they are connected with

57

social institutions, specimens of a type, pieces of a system . . .' When only 1,000 citizens of Manchester are poor, then people seek to explain poverty by reference to personal defects. When 35 per cent of the citizens are said to be living at about the State poverty line, then their predicament cannot be accounted for by personal or community defects alone. People are compelled to accept that the structure of opportunities has collapsed. The American sociologist, C. Wright Mills, noted that 'both the correct statement of the problem and the range of possible solutions require us to consider the economic and political institutions of society and not merely the personal situation and character of a scatter of individuals' and communities. In other words, poverty cannot be explained without reference to the way society is ordered in its class and institutional forms.

(a) The Class Explanation of Poverty.

The poor cannot be considered in isolation from the affluent. To comprehend and explain poverty adequately includes comprehending and explaining affluence. It has been noted how poverty is concentrated particularly amongst the unskilled, amongst social class V, and not in the managerial and professional class I. By acknowledging the different levels in society the class nature of poverty and inequality becomes apparent. A category begins to emerge which stretches across individuals and communities.

What is class? Many people do not believe it exists, or rather like sex, they believe it should not exist. Working as teachers or managers they avoid its reality by proclaiming that everyone is now working-class. It is not easy to argue with people who stand in between the low tide and high tide marks and assume because they tell the sea loudly and confidently not to drown them that it will not. Yet in Britain there are marked and consistent differences in income, occupation and prestige. These distinctions inevitably lead 'to a series of strata consisting of hierarchies or layers distinct from each other'. They reflect 'a set of closely related inequalities of economic condition, power and opportunity'. All the material examined in this book points to the existence of such a reality, and that reality is called class.

There are four factors which clarify and substantiate this linking of poverty and class.

First, there is a need to note the power and inflexibility of the class structure. The class system does not simply reveal marked inequalities in British society. It also possesses a high degree of rigidity. The distribution of power is not only unequal. The problem is made worse by the same groups holding on to power just as others like the poor are denied it. This power and inflexibility is demonstrated in two ways. On the one hand, it is revealed by the presence of a powerful élite which has maintained a dominant role in the running of most major institutions in society. In ways obverse to the poor, members of the élite have a distinctive life style, high occupational position and high status. Educated at public school and Oxbridge, this tiny proportion of the population (only 4 per cent of the population were educated at public school) occupy a vastly disproportionate number of key positions in society. In the late 1970s, for example, 86 per cent of army officers of the rank of major-general or above, 81 per cent of principal judges, 73 per cent of the directors of the largest industrial corporations, 60 per cent of permanent secretaries in the civil service, and 70 per cent of bishops in the Church of England all came from public school backgrounds.

On the other hand, the inflexibility of such an ordering of society is suggested by the fact that this élite has remained intact for many years. According to one researcher 'over a generation or more, despite all efforts to broaden the recruitment base of some significant professions and occupations, the situation does not as yet differ substantially from that which appertained before the war'. The myth of serious movement between classes, that every private has a field-marshal's baton in his pack, is not substantiated by careful research. Between 1953 and

1963, only one in 12 crossed from manual to non-manual groups, and many were married women re-entering employment. The great panacea of education for all has not, in the words of Professor Halsey, 'led to unequivocal evidence of greater fluidity of movement between classes'. There has been 'no significant reductions in class inequalities'. We may always have the poor with us, but we also always have the rich.

Secondly, there is a need to note that the class system results in the denial of access to resources to the poor. Such an inflexible social system means that a small percentage of the affluent population has easy access to resources. The obverse side of the coin results in the poor being denied such access to resources. With regard to health in general, or infant mortality rates in particular, and especially in education, certain social groups have a disproportionately large share of available resources. Given the scarcity of resources, this diminishes the share available to others. The self-interest of the rich at best, and their selfishness at worst, always drives them to defend their hold on resources.

The denial of access to resources to the poor is not only an explanation of poverty in Britain. It equally explains the existence of poor Third World nations in relation to rich First World nations. Those who say we should not bother with the problem of the poor in Britain because they are not poor compared to the poor in India simply evade the root cause of poverty. They cannot see that the explanations of world poverty offered by the Brandt Report and structural explanations of British poverty are part of the same mould. To develop appropriate help for the Third World poor should not be separated from developing structures of help to the poor in Britain. 'We have a double responsibility'.

Thirdly, there is a need to note the influence of the class system on hostile attitudes to the poor. The unskilled manual worker, although only a minority in the population (8 per cent), is part of a society which explains social position significantly in terms of individual skill, qualifications and motivation. It is precisely these work-ethic virtues which result in the unskilled worker being classified in relation to the more established ordering in society. He has no status in his own right, and is always described as the *un*qualified, the *un*skilled, and the *dis*advantaged. The obverse side of a society whose cardinal virtues are skill, thrift and self-reliance is a society which treats with suspicion and hostility those who fall out of work and who are not able to practise these majority virtues. What this means for the lives of the poor has already been noted.

Fourthly, there is a need to note the relationship between class, politics and the maintenance of poverty. The power and persistence of élites in British society when coupled with the powerlessness and persistence of poverty reveals the limited value of the political and civil rights associated with democracy. It demonstrates that in accepting political democracy we 'changed our political garments but not our heart'. The denial to the poor of access to the generally accepted standards of living in health, education, housing, work, income and wealth suggests that a restricted form of political democracy is being used to ensure that the affluent remain affluent and therefore the poor remain poor.

(b) The Institutional Explanation of Poverty.

The way society is ordered contributes in a powerful way to the existence of poverty and privilege. It does so through its class system but also through the workings of its great institutions and in particular the Welfare State and education.

The Welfare State. It has been noted how the Welfare State from the moment of its creation became, through the National Assistance Board, a cause of the poverty which in theory it was supposed to prevent. According to the politicians it was just never practical 'to pay benefits generous enough to prevent want'.

However, the Welfare State is not just a provider of such limited resources as to produce poverty. It also acts as a distributor of advantages and so contributes to the increase of inequality. Over twenty years ago Professor Titmuss, one of the great commentators on the Welfare State, showed how the middle classes do significantly better out of the traditional Welfare State than the poorer groups in society. In addition, four other 'welfare states' have emerged, each significantly reinforcing the process of redistribution to the affluent and away from the poor. The four include: the tax allowance welfare state in which the biggest earners and home owners are the greatest beneficiaries, and which distributes in tax allowances almost as much as the traditional Welfare State (the top 9 per cent of taxpayers earning more than £10,000 a year gained 34 per cent of all mortgage interest tax benefit paid out during 1979–80); the company welfare state paying out pensions, sick pay, insurance, cars, loans, fees for private education and health, with most of this going to the better-paid rather than to the manual workers; the inherited power welfare state which concentrates the ownership of wealth into the hands of a very small number of people significantly dependent on inheritance for their power; and finally, the private market welfare state which enables wealth-owners and higher income earners to buy privileged health and education. These in their turn give their recipients a greater and easier hold on the key resources of work, income and power.

Yet the problem is not just about the way in which the Welfare State(s) distributes resources and how this contributes to the existence of poverty and privilege. That contribution to poverty is also connected to the way in which the Welfare State is funded. The Welfare State is financed from the national insurance contributions of employees and employers, and from the Exchequer. In terms of national insurance contributions, the poorer groups pay a larger proportion of their incomes than do other groups. In terms of the contribution of the Exchequer through taxation, on the one hand, the poor are now bearing a greater burden of direct taxation (as income tax) than the more affluent. On the other hand, the shift to indirect taxation (through VAT) again hits the poor most. The DHSS observed that 'a shift from income tax to commodity taxation would help the rich and hit the poor'. Recent budgets have only exacerbated these trends towards a regressive system of financing a Welfare State which then distributes resources again on a regressive basis. No wonder that a recent observer suggested that the aim of the Welfare State was to 'supplement existing programmes rather than alter fundamentally the status and economic position of the poor in our society'. It reflects a society which has always been more successful at producing poverty than removing it.

Education. Historians of the industrial revolution have long recognized that behind the existence of educational and other measures to combat social problems lay the reality of wealth and its distribution. Those with wealth were able to purchase the educational resource, those without were not. The latter were condemned to a poor education and therefore almost inevitably to poor jobs or unemployment. That contribution of education to inequality and to poverty has persisted to the present day. Educational institutions are as stratified as ever, and the middle classes continue to gain a greater purchase on resources than the poorer groups in the form either of private or higher education. The unskilled are marginalized by an educational system which has never taken them seriously and which shows little sign of doing so. They leave school with no qualifications for the poverty of low-paid employment or of unemployment. Tawney acknowledged that any serious pursuit of a more equal and fair society could never be undertaken as long as great wealth was inherited and private education flourished.

The nature and extent of the class system in Britain and the damaging as well as constructive effects of great institutions combine to provide conditions which make and keep people poor. Poverty is clearly produced by more than the defects of individuals or areas. It is an integral part of the very ordering of society with its powerful self-maintaining properties. That is the conclusion of this examination into why there is poverty in Britain today.

CHAPTER FIVE
How Should We Respond to Poverty?

Living in a period of rapid and extensive change means that any discussion of poverty and what can be done about it would be defective if it did not take into account the two great realities of deindustrialization and unemployment. These complementary forces are so influential in today's society that they justify explanation. By *deindustrialization* is meant the rapid decline of wealth-creating manufacturing industries. That decline can be measured by the alarming fall in manufacturing output (from a 30 per cent increase in the 1960s to a nil to minus growth in the early seventies to early eighties), by a poor record in manufacturing productivity (output per person employed increased in Britain by 5 per cent from 1973–79, but Japan's and West Germany's increased by 30 per cent), by the fall in the numbers employed in manufacturing (which fell from 8.4 million in 1966 to 6.0 million in 1982), by the weakening of manufacturing exports (their value exceeded the value of manufacturing imports by 60 per cent in 1970 but only by 10 per cent in 1979), and by the decline in manufacturing investment (excluding depreciation and replacement needs, real additional investment fell by 43 per cent from 1970 to 1979). Put together, these facts clearly suggest the decline of Britain as a major manufacturing nation at least when compared to its major competitors. By *unemployment* is meant the growth of large-scale unemployment. This officially stood at three million by the end of 1981, but in reality numbered nearer four million if the unemployed on government temporary work schemes and people not registered but wanting work were included. Such unemployment is not only enormous in extent, it is also increasingly long-term. There have been over one million unemployed since 1976, with little likelihood of a reduction to even this figure by 1990. By early 1982 over one million of the total number of unemployed had been without work for over twelve months.

These forces of deindustrialization and unemployment gravely affect the nature and extent of poverty through their effects on the manual worker and especially the unskilled worker. With the decline of British industry, and since manual workers are three times more vulnerable to unemployment than non-manual workers, there were one and a half million manual workers unemployed by 1982 in relationship to a falling total of nine million manual worker jobs. In other words, for every five manual workers in employment there is a surplus of one unemployed manual worker. This means that the continuing unemployment of manual workers is now built into the structures of British industry and society. This structural unemployment has resulted in the creation of a reserve army of unemployed manual workers five times larger than the entire armed forces.

The unskilled manual worker is even more vulnerable than his other manual worker colleagues to the forces of industrial change. It has been noted already how, in the North West, there were 123,642 unemployed general labourers from social class V chasing 181 vacancies, a ratio of 679:1 in contrast to a ratio of 16:1 for unemployed managerial and professional workers. Such figures do suggest that we may be witnessing what C. Wright Mills elsewhere called 'the collapse of the structure of opportunities', but in this case for a whole social class. If this diagnosis is correct it will affect profoundly the extent of poverty in Britain. Not simply does more unemployment mean more poverty particularly for the unskilled workers of social class V; up to 50 per cent of unskilled manual workers and their families were already vulnerable to poverty before the onslaught of unemployment. The gross inequalities existing in society will simply be extended and the predicament of the poor will grow worse. As Britain's national wealth diminishes in relation to that of others through the process of deindustrialization, the entrenched interests of powerful social classes and regions will at least *maintain* their hold on the resources of high incomes and good employment, education, housing and health. Since total resources will be getting relatively smaller, they will only be able to achieve this at the *increasing* expense of the most vulnerable social classes and regions. This will result inevitably in the poor becoming poorer and the rich getting richer.

It is against this backcloth of growing deindustrialization and unemployment, which confirms and accentuates what has been noted about the nature, extent and explanations of poverty that consideration must be given to what can be done about poverty in Britain.

There are three major responses to poverty which need to be examined. They are the individualist, the area, and the structures-of-society responses. In the light of the formula which links analysis (as definition and explanation) with policies, each response explored will relate to the appropriate explanation examined in the previous chapter.

1. THE INDIVIDUALIST RESPONSE.

There are two major types of policy associated with the individualist response: first, policies which treat the individual as guilty but also as the means to economic health, and secondly, policies promoting the practice of caring for the individual.

(a) *Policies treating the individual as guilty but also as the means to economic health.* Developing from the individualist explanation of poverty, these policies attempt to tackle poverty by punishing the idle poor and by encouraging the resourceful person.

There is a long tradition of seeking to prevent poverty by making the position of the poor so uncomfortable as to drive them out of their poverty. Any who then chose to remain poor would suffer the consequences of shame and degradation. Campaigns against scroungers, the manufactured humiliation associated with applying for benefits, and ensuring that the long-term unemployed receive the worst benefits (because otherwise they would find life on the dole more attractive than work) are all part of this classic response to poverty. Nicholls, a nineteenth-century Poor Law Commissioner, described it in these words: 'I wish to see the Poor House looked to with dread by our labouring classes, and the reproach for being an inmate of it extended downwards from Father to Son . . . for without this, where is the needful stimulus to industry?' It is clear from our families' experience and from the surveys examined that this policy of finding the poor guilty and making them feel so has been only too successful. But it does not stimulate them to escape from their poverty for they do not have the power to do this, and so this response is cruel to no purpose.

The individualist policy has not only sought to make poverty unattractive. It has also sought to recognize and encourage the individual's autonomy by freeing him from the restrictions of the State. Increasing incentives by reducing direct taxation, and encouraging economic expansion by privatizing welfare services and therefore putting them back into the market place, are all part of a response which assumes that the good of the individual, the market and society are the same. That is proposed as the way to answer the poverty question.

Attractive as many find this individualist response to poverty, it cannot sort out the problems of poverty as reflected in the forces of deindustrialization and unemployment. It never has. It has been noted already that it was the very powerlessness of individuals in the face of nineteenth-century industrial change which drove good people at least to seriously amend, and at most to seek to replace laissez-faire individualism. Placing parts of the welfare services, health and education into the private sector will only reduce the status of the public sector, let alone recreating the wastefulness of a competition which compelled the collectivizing of these services in the first place. It does seem a pity to have to repeat the mistakes which our forefathers made and tried to overcome.

(b) Policies promoting the practice of caring for the individual.

There is a long and noble tradition of responding by practical caring to what are seen as the problems of individuals. Such philanthropy can take a number of forms varying from a very basic good neighbourliness to a more sophisticated counselling and case-work approach. Both seek to compensate for or amend the deficiencies of problem individuals and families. Practical caring can also be seen in the policies which seek to remedy the individual's lack of skills by various kinds of training provision. Examples of this response include Oxfam's plea for money not to give fish to the world's poor but to teach them how to fish for themselves. The Manpower Services Commission's (MSC) assumption that the major problem of the unemployed unskilled young person is his lack of skill, and that therefore he needs training, is in a similar vein.

Despite the obvious human need to help individuals to survive, this response has clear limitations as a means of combatting the nature and extent of poverty charted in these pages. Private charity and voluntary organizations do not have the resources to combat large-scale *endemic* poverty effectively. Indeed, the amount of charitable effort in the nineteenth-century was a recognition of the limits of self-help in the face of great industrial change. Perhaps even more damaging is the criticism that what the unskilled lack is jobs, the absence of which can never be remedied by any amount of training. This criticism is reflected too in the cry of the poor that what they lack is material resources. It is not the therapy and social tranquillisers often prescribed by well-meaning social workers which they need. Altruism and middle-class reform have grave limits in the face of the pressures of deindustrialization and unemployment. Indeed, some would argue that it is the exhaustion of all these traditional caring concerns and the lack of new ways of caring which significantly explains the persistence of poverty.

2. THE AREA RESPONSE.

Even before the mid-nineteenth century, social commentators began to observe the harmful effects of the Industrial Revolution. They particularly noted their impact on certain urban communities, some of which have remained classic slums to this day. One such slum, Ordsall in Salford, was described by Engels in 1844 in terms of its filth and overcrowding, recognized by Robert Roberts in 1914, and then by Graham Markall in 1980. It is not surprising that there has emerged a response to poverty which concentrates resources on such areas. It has taken the form of community work and government policy-making.

Community work is essentially the grossing-up onto a community level of the social work response to individual people and families. The problem individual becomes the problem community to be given important help. Such assistance can vary from setting up pre-school play groups to organizing and servicing self-help tenants' associations.

Government area policies have recognized the particular vulnerability of certain regions and locations to industrial change and deprivation. Since the 1960s this approach has grown especially in the fields of housing, education and industry. It reached its climax in 1980 with the introduction of Enterprise Zones, one of which includes part of Engel's Ordsall.

The recognition that certain communities are more vulnerable to poverty is obviously important. Yet it cannot fully engage the forces of deindustrialization and unemployment which so powerfully affect particular social classes stretching across and beyond the designated areas. It is therefore not surprising that Educational Priority Areas, with their expensive special payments to teachers and schools, have had no discernible results. The influence of forces outside the classroom in the form of bad housing, low income and pay, and now high unemployment, far outweigh the limited value of school-room education. Working either with particular communities or individuals has also been susceptible to the problems of duplication, fragmentation and a wide diversity in quality of service. The success of the successful community worker in attracting resources into a disadvantaged community is always done partly at the expense of other equally disadvantaged communities.

Perhaps the most damaging criticism of the area response to poverty is that by its concentration on problem communities it misses out a vital part of the equation. To adapt the words of Tawney, what thoughtful advantaged areas call the problem of the disadvantaged area, disadvantaged areas with equal justice call the problem of the advantage area. The area response to poverty is not adequately able to engage those forces which lie outside and yet powerfully shape poor communities. It does not check the undue power of the affluent. With such a defective equation, it is not surprising that despite its value for highlighting some of the features of poverty, it cannot produce answers adequate for dealing with them.

3. THE STRUCTURES-OF-SOCIETY RESPONSE.

If poverty is about deindustrialization and unemployment, and yet about *more than that*, and if adequate responses to poverty are about individualist and area policies, and yet about *more than that*, then what does '*the more than that*' require of us? To make any real progress in answering this question requires facing up to three preliminary truths: first, the truth that since poverty is a national phenomenon then effective poverty policies need to be at least as comprehensive in their scope. If adequate explanations of poverty move beyond individual and community defects into class and institutional explanations, then presumably adequate responses to poverty must do the same. They must engage the very ordering and structures of society. They must become, in President Johnson's words, a 'national war on poverty. Our objective—total victory'.

Secondly, there is the truth that old dialectics are of little use in the face of new realities. If the forces of deindustrialization and unemployment are symptomatic of a radical change occurring in our society and in its relationship to other societies, then it is probably most unlikely that their impact on poverty can be faced up to effectively by traditional means. As William Cobbett noted with reference to the unreformed House of Commons in 1822, there is little value in renovating a machine which has never worked well. The need is for a radical 'alteration in the machine' itself.

Thirdly, there is the truth that politics are for people and so a way is needed to test the actual *effectiveness* of the practical concern for the poor and vulnerable in society. Since the impact of industrial change on the manual worker and on poverty is so comprehensive in its effects, policies to control industrial change and counter poverty need to be equally comprehensive. Yet the Judaeo-Christian tradition has a very specific concern for the vulnerable in society. It is therefore important to develop a test of policies which although comprehensive in its scope, is particularly sensitive to the needs of the poor.

Such a criterion can be formed by combining the insights of Patrick Jenkin and R.H. Tawney. The former developed 'family impact statements'; that is tests of the effects on family life of any proposed legislation. The latter became convinced that 'the only sound test of a policy or system is its practical effect on the lives of human beings'. By putting the two together in relation to the poor there emerges the criterion of *poverty impact statements* which test policies by their practical effect on the lives of the ordinary person in general and the poor in particular.

Given these three preliminary truths there is little point in discussing traditional economic and social policies as answers to the problem of poverty. Old dialectics cannot cope with new realities. Instead, consideration should be given to three key areas which lie at the heart of the changes affecting society and which bear directly on the position of the poor. The removal of poverty and the creation of a viable and just society will inevitably require taking these three areas of work, income and social fabric seriously.

(a) *The nature of industry and work.* Tawney became very clear that the fundamental cause of the present malaise was not the issue of poverty but lay rather at the heart of industry. There is much to be said for such a view. Industry is perhaps the greatest force shaping both society and poverty. It is intimately associated with the social class system, based as the latter is on occupational status and deeply infecting industrial life. There is nothing more nonsensical and inefficient than the sight of a manual worker with 30 years experience and service working in the same factory as his 18 year old daughter and seeing the significantly better hours, holidays, sick pay, pensions and canteen facilities which the latter automatically inherits as a non-manual secretarial worker. The low pay earned by many workers in industry is also one of the main causes of poverty. The fact that the relationship between bottom earners on poor incomes and the average has remained unchanged over 100 years inevitably suggests the connivance of employers and trade unionists at the persistence of low pay. Any policies to combat poverty have therefore to take these industrial matters seriously. What this could involve can be seen in the following selection of four industrial priorities for action:

(i) Given the impact of deindustrialization and unemployment on manual workers there is a desperate immediate need to create jobs for them. The construction industry and the public service sector (including caring for the elderly and mentally sick in their homes and communities) could provide work for the unemployed which is valuable in its own right and in the eyes of society. It is nonsense to allow millions to live in bad housing and squalid dirty environments, while paying at least £4,500 for each of the three million unemployed.

(ii) Deindustrialization must be reversed because it reduces the funds available for the Welfare State and diminishes the quality of life for all. To maintain industrial viability will require a host of measures but it will mean particularly improving the poor record of investment in British industry. The problem is not lack of personal or institutional wealth, but a failure to make use of it for the benefit of the public good. Increasing competitiveness will also require improving productivity and introducing new technologies. Wages too would presumably not continue to grow unrelated to wealth creation. Instead they would become part of a comprehensive policy to maintain viability, part of whose function would be to provide the resources for new work creation. None of this could be effectively achieved without advances also being made in the other two areas to be examined of income and social fabric.

(iii) There can be no serious attack on poverty without a serious attack on the problem of large-scale and persisting low pay. It was years ago that the Prices and Incomes Board stated the only sensible policy-objective when it declared: 'it must be the aim of society, if it can afford to set a basic standard of provision such as the supplementary benefit level, to try and ensure that as a minimum workers who are reasonably fit and exercise common prudence, have the opportunity to achieve a significantly higher standard of living than this'.

(iv) With the end of full employment and with the active labour force diminishing as a proportion of the total population, there is a crucial need to promote discussion and change practices with regard to the attitudes to and understanding of work and its contribution to the life of society and of individuals. What is and should be the relationship of work to paid employment and to purposeful activity (like voluntary and domestic work) which is not paid? How can the former and its necessary contribution to economic viability be maintained whilst increasingly recognizing the latter and ensuring all receive minimum adequate incomes? Such a change needs more than a changed attitude to those not earning wages. It also suggests a far-reaching 'transformation of the scale of productive and non-productive values'. Without such a debate and accompanying changes in policy (towards, say, reducing overtime and encouraging parts of the so-called black economy), a view of work will persist which is not commensurate with the reality of the situation. Inaccurate perceptions and attitudes to the unemployed in particular and to the poor in general will continue to infect society.

In other words, the demands for work creation, industrial viability, the disappearance of low pay, and changed understandings of work will make the traditional dialectics of economic and industrial life increasingly redundant. They will drive people away from sterile arguments over public ownership or free markets, or over whether to pursue economic growth or oppose it (the former has not improved the relative position of the poor over 100 years, and the latter could impoverish everyone).

(b) *The importance of income and its distribution*. The problem of low incomes, like the creation of wealth, lies at the heart of the poverty issue. The poor need what the affluent have always had, money. (This does not detract from the recognition that poor access to housing, education and health also produces poverty). The struggle for a level of income sufficient to raise people out of poverty has long been part of movements for justice in Church and society. In a period of low growth, the level and distribution of income becomes an even more important issue. There are two main aspects to this struggle.

The first and most significant is the need to ensure that all receive an adequate income. With the comparative affluence of the majority, however, this now means that tying minimum incomes to mere subsistence levels is an increasingly insufficient response. The emergence of earnings-related benefits and benefits linked to cost of living increases are a recognition of this principle of a more generous minimum. The possible introduction of a statutory minimum wage is another option to be considered. (The experiment with the latter in New Zealand and Australia is interestingly also associated with a more egalitarian distribution of earnings compared with the position in Britain). This concern for securing adequate incomes is not only necessary for the maintenance and possibility of a decent life. If successful it would also make available to all that *economic resisting power* so essential for the exercise of freedom and responsibility. It is this lack of resources which promotes the powerlessness of the poor in relation to the power of the affluent. It is the denial to millions of access to property in the form of reasonable incomes, wealth, housing, education, health and employment which is so damaging to the body politic. As Bacon noted nearly 400 years ago, wealth like manure is most effective when spread as widely as possible.

Second, however, is the need to recognize that the question of minimum incomes and wages cannot properly be considered in isolation from proposals for maximum incomes and wages. To raise the former to a decent level will inevitably reduce the proportion of national wealth available to the latter. It will inevitably lead into the whole debate about the redistribution of income and wealth on a more equitable basis. Debates over adequate subsistence levels in our kind of society cannot properly be separated from debates over differentials. The sooner this is honestly faced by the powers that be in society in general and in industry and the trade unions in particular, the sooner poverty will be vanquished. Inevitably this will mean promoting open discussion about what fair and realistic differentials are acceptable to society. However this debate develops it will presumably wish to seriously reduce the post-tax differentials between the top and bottom incomes from their present indecent 20:1 to 7:1 or even to 3:1. Bland announcements as from heaven that captains of industry are to receive increases double what an unemployed private and his family receive in total will then be deservedly cast into the dustbin. The pursuit of justice for the poor can never be separated from the pursuit of a smaller proportionate share of total national resources by higher income groups.

To address the question of minimum and maximum incomes is inevitably about more than a question of redistribution. It invariably leads into a discussion of the national framework needed for the yearly distribution of earned and unearned (benefits) income. This would have the additional advantage of eroding the prejudices arising from an undue division between those who earn their income from employment and all those, like the elderly, sick and unemployed, who are dependent on the State for the means of life. New understandings of the changing realities of work will demand no less. The question of minimum and maximum incomes cannot be separated, too, from the reform of what is essentially a regressive taxation policy. For example, between 1960–1 and 1979–80 the proportion of income paid in tax and national insurance by a single person on average earnings rose by 57 per cent; for a couple with two children the increase was 302 per cent. Progressive incomes policies, when accompanied by regressive taxation policies, are clearly unproductive incompatibles.

(c) *The importance of the social fabric and tissue.* Combatting poverty must always be about more than facing up to the problems of individuals and their communities. It must always include addressing the issues of social class and institutional life. Of course any effective consideration of work and income will inevitably have a direct bearing on both issues. Class is closely related to occupation, and industry and the Welfare State are the two main providers of income. Yet there is something about class and the life of institutions which stretches beyond the world of work and the provision of incomes and which greatly influences the very heart of the fabric and tissue of society. There is something about the predicament of the poor which can only be explained by the presence of attitudes and organizations prejudicial to their interests. To face up to this and to surmount it in a critical and practical way is a crucial part of any programme attempting to combat poverty.

In order to do this, there are three areas of life which need to be addressed and which allow a hold to be obtained on this more intangible reality of social fabric and tissue. They are the divisions in society, the institutions of the Welfare State, and the promotion of participation.

The divisions in society. The class system causes immense damage to the whole fabric of British life, and clearly is a major factor behind the persistence of large-scale poverty. The erosion of poverty can only be achieved if a whole series of ways are found to reduce those great social divisions which not only separate people and communities from each other but also foster feelings and positions of superiority and inferiority between them. The CBI has welcomed the gradual removal of harmful barriers between management and workers which established centres of privilege even in canteens and urinals. The erosion of social forms of apartheid also extends to challenging the manufactured divisions between council and private housing estates, concentrating as they do particular classes into particular ghettos. It presumably includes too the severe questioning of the persistence and growth of privileged education and health care. Serious attempts to eradicate poverty can never be made without eating into the obvious power of élites and their imbalanced purchase on valuable resources in all these sectors of life. To allow the persistence of such undue freedom to some inevitably detracts from the freedom of others. Etons and Harley

Streets will always mean Liverpool 8s and Grunwicks. It was perhaps with this in mind that Gladstone, as a great Liberal, opposed the right of the affluent to buy into the army and civil service in the nineteenth-century. The time will surely come when the right to purchase privileged education and health will also be discarded. There are some things which should never be open to purchase in a good society.

The institutions of the Welfare State. Since the Welfare State and benefit system produce poverty and contribute to inequality, the latter's abolition can only be achieved by the reform of the Welfare State. This requires facing up to at least two crunch issues. First, it will probably mean moving from an overdependence on a regressive national insurance contributory Welfare State (that is, from benefits earned as of right and paid for by national insurance contributions), to a progressive social security tax Welfare State. Unlike the former, the latter would be linked to a person's capacity to pay. This would remove, for example, the nonsense of the unemployed having after twelve months, to move off the much better unemployment benefit (to which they have contributed through national insurance payments) onto the much lower supplementary benefit basic rate (to which they have contributed through taxation). The position originally advocated by Lloyd George would then be reached, that 'gradually the obligation of the state to find labour or sustenance will be realised and honourably interpreted. Insurance will then be unnecessary'. It would then be possible to move to a Welfare State covering all citizens and all sectors of life, with income provided as of right without being tied to contribution or means test. The stigma, expense and social control associated with the latter would be removed for ever from the social policies of an increasingly post-industrial society.

Secondly, and strategically complementing the first, the funding of the Welfare State needs to move gradually to a more redistributive taxation policy. This would have less emphasis on indirect taxation (VAT) and more on direct taxation. The reform of the latter would presumably involve the reform of the four additional 'welfare states' (the tax allowance, the company, the inherited power, and the private market welfare states). It would also include a vertical redistribution from the more affluent to the disadvantaged, and a horizontal redistribution across people's life-spans to give them more resources in their young-family and old-age stages when they are more vulnerable to poverty.

The promotion of participation. Removing social divisions and opening up institutions to the poorer members of society are an essential part of the whole debate about increasing the say of all groups and individuals over those great matters which affect their lives. Enlarging the ability to participate is a quite crucial part of the struggle to overcome poverty. Poverty so powerfully isolates the poor both from society and the opportunity to have a say in it that eroding their powerlessness must always occupy a central part of any policies to combat poverty.

It has already become evident how industry and incomes (as economic resisting power) provide important ways in which power can be dispersed more widely and resources found for its exercise. Yet the opportunity and ability to participate in decision-making is about having a say in far more than industry and the operating of the Welfare State. It has to occur equally in the local neighbourhood where people need to be helped to exercise more control over their lives. Robert Holman illustrates what this means when he cites the account of 'a passive, poverty-stricken woman ... dwelling in slum council property with a mentally-ill husband and a large young family. She had no prospects of re-housing in better accommodation because of her "low" housekeeping standards. The dwelling's toilet, an outdoor one, was unusable in wet weather due to holes in the roof which the council, despite her many requests, did not repair. The woman felt there was nothing she could do but accept the council's decision. She became a committee member of a local neighbourhood group and ran one of its playgroups.

Here she saw members handling officials in a different manner. She realized she did not always have to bow meekly to the off-putting responses of clerks in the Housing Department. She thus adopted a more forceful pose and insisted on seeing the housing manager, refusing to leave the building until she did so. This achieved, she threatened to go to the press unless the repairs were made. The toilet was speedily mended'. Community action leading to tenants' associations or welfare rights' groups does allow the poor to speak for themselves. The importance of such a development cannot be emphasized enough. There is nothing worse than middle-class groups and leaders forever speaking for the poor. They never overcome the problem that 'those who do not speak for themselves are not likely to be effectively spoken for by others'. Yet increasing the power of the poor in these ways will again be achieved only by reducing the power of the affluent.

If A.H. Halsey is correct in his diagnosis of our social ills, then the fact has to be addressed that 'we have an economy that does not release our energies, a polity that does not secure our trust, and a culture which does not sufficiently attract our affections'. Poverty is an integral and particular part of that general malaise. Any effective cure requires a whole series of policy and attitude changes, pre-eminent amongst which must surely be the reform of institutional life. It was with this aim in mind that Halsey observed that 'the problem is to discover, to establish, and to strengthen those social institutions that will encourage and foster the kind of relations between people that are desired'. The reform of the Welfare State, the erosion of élites and the promotion of participation are essential parts of such a programme.

The forces of deindustrialization and unemployment as they affect the lives of the poor reveal the limitations of individualist and area-based policies. Yet they do not thereby invalidate all the insights contained within these policies. So complex is the issue of poverty that no single policy can ever remove its blight from society. Although changing the structures of society is the most important objective for policies to combat poverty this does not exclude (and indeed must be complemented by) proper account being taken of the insights revealed in the individualist and area responses to poverty. The removal of poverty is about addressing its causes as they affect individuals, areas and structures. Each has a contribution to make to the development of adequate responses to poverty. Yet these assertions should never be allowed to modify the priority which needs to be given to structures-of-society responses to poverty. The criterion of policies which tests their adequacy by their practical effect on the lives of the ordinary person in general and the poor in particular requires no less than such an emphasis.

PART THREE

Perspectives on the Human
Predicament:
Towards a Better Understanding
and Living.

Development of the Argument

As the shape of an argument unfolds it sometimes becomes clear that its logic is driving one into new ways of looking at things. This happened during the writing of this book and especially in the third and final part. So important was the change for the argument that what happened needs to be described.

The book was begun according to a plan which divided into two sections. In the first, the intention was to present definitions and explanations of poverty with their implications for practice. This was done with the addition of representative case studies and reasons why the poor should be taken seriously. The assumption was that the aim of the second section would be to examine the implications of this more secular analysis and policies for the Churches. The first section would stand in its own right and perhaps be of interest to a wider than Christian audience. The second would appeal only to the Churches.

As these last two chapters were approached it became clear that the drift of the argument had changed and altered the whole tenor of the book. If poverty is as entrenched in society as it appears to be, and if it is reinforced by the forces of deindustrialization and unemployment, will the ways to overcome poverty suggested in Chapter Five be adequate? Faced by this question, it became obvious that the analysis and policies examined in the first five chapters, indispensable as they are for any adequate facing up to poverty, would never be sufficient to remove poverty from society. They would not overcome the negative and seemingly perennial attitudes to disadvantaged people which have always been found in societies in which poverty and affluence abound.

Before writing this book I had assumed that an analysis of poverty and approaches to it would show the Church how to respond to poverty. But this last section now assumes a new significance, because it has become clear that current approaches to poverty are insufficient. If therefore new material can be found then it could be indispensable for any seeking to face up to poverty. In other words, what the Church can draw out of its traditions may contain insights of value for society as a whole. Indeed, the limitations of the responses described so far suggest that what might have been thought of initially as additional matters for the Church's eyes only may now become central to what can be done about poverty. This would be wholly in accordance with the understanding that a truly Christian response to God moves people closer to human realities.

Such a conclusion has important implications for the Church as well as society. It means that it can be authentically and properly involved in the poverty question because it has significant insights and experiences to offer to its solution. It means that material indispensable for any adequate involvement with the poor can be supplemented by material illuminated by the Christian tradition in ways invaluable to both Christians and people of goodwill and good sense alike. By addressing the Church over what the implications of this analysis of poverty are for human fulfilment, for Christian practice, and for thought and a way of life, it might be possible for the whole of society to move towards remedying the deficiencies in the more traditional analyses and responses.

CHAPTER SIX

What the Poor Mean for a New View of What We Are.

It was deep in the Scottish countryside that what it means to be a human being in contemporary urban life was brought home to me. Perhaps strange for such a venue but not for such a subject, the issue was raised at a conference about the nature of working life in the 1980s. After a long debate about deindustrialization and unemployment the conference began to discuss whether there was something about work which was necessary for human fulfilment. If so, did this mean work as paid employment or was there emerging a wider understanding of work as purposive activity covering the domestic and voluntary spheres of life as well as wage-labour? Was there indeed a question behind such questions which was about what was involved in people being people and what was necessary for their growth to any kind of fulfilment.

It is to answer precisely this deeper question, that the issue of poverty drives people. A study of the predicament of the poor should reveal what they miss about life, and therefore what they really need in order to live it, in the same way that an examination of the unemployed can reveal what they miss about work and therefore what they really *need*. To begin to answer this more underlying question might indeed allow people to cut through much of the dead wood which surrounds contemporary debates about poverty and affluence.

It is important to address what makes people people,

and what it demands of us for their fulfilment for two additional reasons. In the first place prudence requires it. Unless it is possible to show that poverty affects everyone, then it will never be possible to gain the necessary support to make the far-reaching changes needed in society to eradicate poverty. If the problem of the poor can be shown to be essentially about the problem of what is necessary for human fulfilment, then that is presumably a matter which affects everyone. None can remain aloof for too long from questions relating to the fulfilment of their own being. It may be that the only way to persuade the affluent majority in the middle classes and South East to take the disadvantaged minority seriously is to face the underlying question about the nature of our humanity as it is raised by the issue of poverty. Without their votes and continuing support no real lasting progress can be made.

In the second place, to face what is meant by our humanity may also allow people to find ways of overcoming some of the limitations associated with the ideal of equality. Arguments for and against equality are so often and so clearly part of yesterday's dialectics that they seriously impede the search for solutions to the problem of today's poverty. Yet since relativities are so central to an adequate understanding of poverty ways do need to be found to allow as many people and interests as possible to face up to some of the fundamental matters traditionally connected with the pursuit of equality. A proper understanding of what it means to be a person may enable this to happen by moving beyond the normally restrictive views of equality.

These deficiencies in more traditional analyses and responses drive us to consider what is the essential humanity of people in two ways. First, what does an understanding of poverty suggest is essential for the pursuit of human fulfilment? Secondly, what does this in turn mean on the one hand for a proper estimate of what is materially necessary for human fulfilment, and on the other hand for ways of moving beyond the concept of equality?

88

1. WHAT IS ESSENTIAL FOR HUMAN FULFILMENT?

There has always been a debate over what the poor need yet lack, and this has always been linked to the struggle to determine what is necessary for life in society. Both drive people to consider the question of what is meant by being human. For example, by what criteria is it decided that the poor are diminished in relation to others? Both, too, suggest the importance of developing an understanding of what is needed for human fulfilment. Involvement with poverty offers precisely such an opportunity to define and promote what it means and can mean to be a person in today's society.

This can be done by looking at experience in the different but related field of unemployment. There is, for instance, a way of looking at what the unemployed lack but need which suggests a profile of what is necessary about work for people. To look at what the poor lack but need may also similarly suggest a profile of what is necessary for human living in our kind of society. If this is attempted then there are two important features about being human which emerge out of such a study. They centre on the availability of resources and the opportunity to develop relationships.

The availability of resources. The experience of poverty focusses attention on the poor's lack of resources. The poor are poor because they lack access to reasonable levels of income, employment, health, housing and education. Without such access, the enhancement of life is rarely possible. To live a full life can normally only be achieved on the basis of a security which is nearly always associated with a reasonable access to the resources of income, employment, health, housing and education. The *ability to maintain a viable life* is an essential prerequisite for the development of a more fulfilled life.

Of course, there are always exceptional people who live fulfilled lives with limited resources and in the most disadvantageous surroundings. Yet they are surely the exceptions from which generalizations should never be made. For most people living in poverty the unremitting living from hand to mouth is rather productive of a constant stress which saps all vitality and destroys all hope. For them poverty always diminishes, it never enhances. It gradually and systematically poisons every sphere of their daily lives from their physical and mental health to their most intimate relationships.

To give the poor access to the basic resources for living in an urban society would at least overcome these insuperable obstacles to the pursuit of any kind of fulfilment. It would give them, too, a stake in society by enabling realistic choices to be made and plans for the future to be laid with hope. The ability to have some choice in such mundane matters as the food you eat is an essential forerunner of not simply exercising the vote but also feeling that in casting it you may be able to affect your life. To be able to plan ahead is always dependent upon that often unconscious assurance which comes from having such sufficient resources behind you as to free you from paying anxious attention to them. Without resources people rapidly lose that vital sense of being able to change their lot. They lose the ability to have a say in their lives. They lose the economic resisting power which is often a key part of the ability to organize and have access to power. A more equal access to what resources there are, is an essential part of what it means to be human with any hope of achieving fulfilment.

The opportunity to develop relationships. To be able to have a proper say in all those matters which affect one's life and make it worth living is indeed the vital link between resources and relationships. Without economic resisting power and its ability to encourage and sustain relationships, proper participation and therefore full citizenship becomes an unrealizable hope. The problem of the poor is not simply that they lack resources but as a result they also lack the ability to participate effectively in the social life of society. Their poverty deeply affects their relationships within their family and with the outside world, and both in turn profoundly influence their estimate of themselves. The stress caused by the unending struggle to make ends meet inevitably corrodes family relationships; lack of finance and suitable clothing soon prohibits active involvement in the social life of a community; the stigma associated with poverty is only fuelled by the dehumanizing treatment often meted out to the poor by officials.

There should be no surprise that the cumulative effect of all these damaged relationships is the production of attitudes of superiority to the poor and deference by the poor. Tawney's most damaging criticism of the post-war Labour Government was that it had done 'little to remove from wage-earners (the) sense that they belong to a subordinate class'. It is that sense and these attitudes which harm and diminish the humanity of poor and affluent alike. There is no greater truth than the reality that when one is diminished all are diminished.

Why is this so? Surely because to talk of human fulfilment is to talk of what makes people more, or less, human, and one of the key matters which distinguishes the former from the latter is the ability to form creative relationships. What people *share* with each other in their relationships is a fundamental part of their humanity; it is a powerful recognition that 'the most important aspect of human beings is not the difference of circumstance, income and race, or even of character and intelligence by which they are divided, but the common humanity which unites them'. Poverty is essentially a rejection and negation of such a belief and reality. It therefore suggests that at the heart of the commitment to the essential humanity of people must be a readiness to seek the spread of realistic opportunities to develop free and equal relationships across the boundaries of self, family, neighbourhood and class.

To promote a view of what it means to be human which includes proper access to resources and relationships is to do more than point to a new understanding of our humanity. It also provides the *motives* for accomplishing that change which is so essential for a successful struggle against poverty. It does this by offering a proper view of the person which is not overridden by an unbalanced emphasis on either community or individualism, but is based on a view of people-in-their-relationships. That view has two aspects. On the one hand, it affirms the importance of a person as a person, and not a person as defined by his or her occupational role or place in society. It promotes a view of society in which 'money and position count for less, and the quality of human personalities for more'. On the other hand, it also asserts that although a person does not live by bread alone he clearly does not live without it and all the collaborative effort needed to supply it.

It is these two aspects of our humanity which generate human-centred imperatives for concern and change. Whilst rejecting 'the tedious vulgarities of income and social position' they also promote a view of the person which stretches beyond but also always leads to a concern for the poor. They suggest that fundamental values in society must ultimately be evaluated not 'by their economic advantage but by the type of individual character and the style of social existence fostered by them'. They provide a means for all to engage the major causes of poverty. They offer a way to seize the imagination of every citizen which offers the only basis for translating policies to remove poverty into practice.

2. THE IMPORTANCE FOR HUMAN FULFILMENT OF MATERIAL RESOURCES AND GOING BEYOND EQUALITY.

The examination of the implications of poverty for what it means to be human has concentrated on the importance of resources and relationships for human living. Both have connections with the two traditional definitions of poverty as subsistence and relative poverty. Yet a consideration of resources and relationships moves people beyond these classic but problematic formulations about poverty. Such a movement should not surprise us. The challenge of deindustrialization and unemployment has already suggested the importance of finding new ways of facing up to underlying questions. What this means is revealed by looking further at resources and relationships as two integral parts of what it means for people to be fully human today.

(a) Beyond traditional definitions of human need.

Without reasonable access to material resources most people cannot grow into the fuller maturity which is so intimately a part of human fulfilment. In society today, income is the most important of these resources although in no way does this detract from the increasing significance for living of health, education and housing.

Most moralists and Christians underestimate this contribution of income to human life. At best they give it a purely instrumental value as the means for purchasing the essentials of life. At worst, and indeed normally, they regard it with moral suspicion. Their view of what is necessary for human fulfilment has centred instead on the human spirit, on the virtues of freedom, courage and creativity but often detached from the realities of ordinary life. They have rarely made moral sense of the value of income for human living.

The understanding of the poor beginning to emerge from this analysis, corrects this moral imbalance in three ways. First, it reveals the supreme importance of adequate incomes for sustaining any kind of normal and moral life *in contemporary society*. Survey after survey has shown that what the poor lack most is money. To neglect that reality is to base attitudes, theories and policies on defective premises. Secondly, it points to the importance of economic resisting power for movement towards fuller lives. Without such a power-base it becomes virtually impossible to have any effective say over matters which either personally affect one's life or the running of society as a whole. Thirdly, it suggests that a concern for incomes

93

is an essential and proper vehicle through which values and preferences are promoted. Money as adequate benefits and wages becomes 'a symbol for a society which enables a man to live his life without fear of poverty and family disaster. Other things are as important as freedom from want. But a society that guards its members from want is likely to do its other tasks well. Social security has thus become a touchstone for the future'. It recognizes income as the supremely relevant moral currency for a wage society.

If income is so important for understanding what it means to be fully human, then what would an adequate basic income for all amount to? Such an understanding of income has to take account of at least two things. On the one hand, it needs to recognize that any estimate of income levels must relate to generally accepted standards in a particular society at a particular time. On the other hand, it needs to accept that a basic income is preferable to past and present concerns for minimum incomes. A concern for minimum standards inevitably generates a minimalist view of humanity which is detrimental to us all. A basic income guaranteed for everyone provides an essential base from which human fulfilment can be pursued. It does not guarantee fulfilment but at least it makes it possible.

What does such a basic income mean? It suggests an income sufficient to guarantee physical survival, to give people the basic means for making and carrying out decisions, and to allow the formation of free and equal relationships within the family and society. In other words it would provide the generally accepted standards of food, clothing, housing and heating, and the ability to partici-pate in the normal activities of that society. It would enable a person to live a self-respecting life as 'a matter of right not grace'.

A basic income suggests, too, the importance of developing detailed and realistic costings of all the matters which are essential for any kind of pursuit of human fulfilment in contemporary society. Such a costing will inevitably relate to more than the traditional poor. It will also need to take account of lower one-income families with young children who are often vulnerable to poverty even when on incomes of £5–6000 per annum. It will mean, too, replacing the costings of Rowntree, Beveridge and Supplementary Benefit with the more accurate estimates of income needs currently being developed by people like Piachaud and Townsend. But it will also mean in all probability developing a form of payment which combines income payment with a taxation system. Various ways of achieving this have been discussed over the years. For example, it could be achieved by guaranteeing to every citizen through a negative income tax system certain cash benefits. If the allowed benefits even with the addition of earnings are less than a certain level then instead of paying tax you would receive benefits sufficient to take you up to the accepted base-line. Everyone would therefore receive a basic non-means-tested income to which for example, part-time earnings could be added. (It is a major nonsense that the retired are allowed to earn significant sums and dignity in addition to their basic pensions, while the long-term unemployed remain inactive and in penury because they are essentially limited to their supplementary benefit).

(b) Beyond traditional understandings of equality in relationships.

If the pressure of growing poverty and rapid industrial change is questioning old ways of putting and doing things, then how can we move beyond traditional ideals and values like equality? Move beyond them we must, since so often, and especially in the case of equality, they produce either-or stances which fuel those divisions associated with the existence of poverty in an affluent society. Yet any movement forward would be unwise to neglect equality's emphasis on the quality of relationships between people and communities. How therefore can ways be found to foster relationships between social groups, areas and individuals which both avoid and reduce divisions and promote common concerns? How can people learn to handle together those redistributions necessary to initiate and sustain such changed relationships?

Some of the answers to these questions have begun to emerge from this study of poverty. An examination of the predicament of the poor in an affluent society suggests an understanding of what it means to be human which is relevant to poor and affluent alike. It includes three important points about relationships and how they can be encouraged to develop which could contain truths about relationships which move beyond values like equality.

First, the emerging understanding of what makes people people asserts the supreme importance of men and women as human beings above any recognition of them in relation to their occupation or income. It points to a view of people which moves through and yet always beyond material resources. It therefore emphasizes that essential humanity which all men and women share. In no way contradicting the reality of the individual, it rather affirms 'not only that exceptional men should be free to exercise their exceptional power, but that common men should be free to make the most of their common humanity'.

Secondly, this understanding of people underwrites the importance of certain values traditionally associated with promoting their humanity, but fashions them through the realities of ordinary life. For example, it defines freedom as having the resources to choose; it defines it in terms of increasing 'the range of alternatives open to ordinary people, and the capacity of the latter to follow their own preferences in choosing between them'. Such access to resources and relationships inevitably requires a more equitable sharing of opportunities if people are to grow into individual and social fulfilment. It requires, with regard to income distribution, the recognition of minimum and maximum income levels. By reformulating in these ways traditional values like freedom and equality, this understanding of an essential humanity also allows people to avoid not simply some of the conflicting views centred on these two values but also that wasteful demand to be committed to either one or the other. It is neither particularly helpful or accurate to argue that liberty is more important than equality, or vice versa. A view of the essential humanity of people is needed which moves through and beyond both.

Thirdly, this understanding of people shows the vital importance of finding ways to redistribute access to resources. Although individuals 'differ profoundly . . . in capacity and character', they are equally entitled 'as human beings to consideration and respect'. The well-being of a society is therefore only likely to be increased 'if it so plans its organization that, whether their powers are great or small, all its members may be *equally* enabled to make the best of such powers as they possess'. The redistribution of access to employment, housing, education, income and wealth can mean nothing less than this.

In each of these three points about relationships ways are offered of translating problems associated with poverty into ideals and values associated with promoting the fulfilment of men and women. They offer everyone the opportunity to form purposes in life, to engage in relationships, and accordingly to nourish self-development. They move beyond values like equality to a view of relationships increasingly influenced by a growing commitment to a wider and more common good based on our understanding of humanity. They translate what are fundamentally religious and moral matters into today's society through categories which emerge from taking the poor seriously. They offer to all a view of what people really are and can be.

Facing up to poverty and industrial change has driven us to examine their implications for an understanding of essential humanity. To address such an underlying issue in this way clearly affects a whole range of matters. For example, it confirms the importance of the reasons why we are involved with poverty, based as they are on the nature and significance of people. It suggests too, the need to re-formulate the motivation and shape of practical caring and what it means for society. Both will be discussed in the next chapter. However, perhaps the most important implication is for the Christian understanding of what is involved in people being people in contemporary society. Clearly, a Christian anthropology will include far more than what this study reveals. Yet what it has indicated is the supreme importance for people of the availability of resources and the opportunity to develop relationships. That understanding has been based upon the reality of actual human experience and not upon abstract theories or false perceptions and attitudes.

To reach this conclusion is of profound theological significance. For the importance of these assertions about basic humanity and its fulfilment is derived for Christians from the understanding that Christian belief and discipleship are concerned precisely with the realities conveyed by these assertions about resources and relationships. It is this belief and these realities which invest the assertions with a supreme significance. *It is therefore through them, and indeed principally through them, that God is to be found and served*. Addressing them in this belief is what Christianity and Church life must now be about.

The effect of this conclusion on Christian anthropology is far-reaching. It means that the assertions about the importance of resources and relationships for human living should now be considered in relation to all the central images which make up the Christian view of man. The traditional two-fold belief that people are made in God's image and people are also sinners needs unpacking into the current scene with the help of these contemporary assertions. Such an approach to the understanding of what it means to be human becomes a more comprehensive and realistic assessment of the nature and potential of people in relation to today's pressing social and human problems. Without an analysis of the poor and the development of the test of 'poverty impact statements' that conclusion would neither have been reached nor maintained. That is why the poor must be taken seriously. Without them none will attain to a full understanding and defence of what it means to be human.

CHAPTER SEVEN

What the Poor Mean for the Practice of the Emerging Church

What should the Church do about poverty? There is an obvious straightforward answer which points to practical caring schemes, support for inner urban area churches, and experimental forms of ministry. Indeed, there is even an emerging revolutionary rhetoric which would talk of the Church standing in solidarity with the poor against their oppressors whether they be multinationals or Mrs Thatcher. Almost all the growing debate in the Church about poverty is represented in these two kinds of response.

Yet, admirable as these traditional answers may once have been, they are increasingly inadequate and unhelpful in the light of what is now happening to society in general and to the poor in particular. There is now a real possibility that Britain is entering a period of major change which will require people to develop new ways of thinking and practising. To pursue old responses in the face of changing realities and understandings would be like putting hard-earned money on a three-legged horse. Christians are surely driven to do far more, given what poverty demands of them both in analysis and practice and in their belief in God and commitment to discipleship.

To work on this agenda will inevitably affect the shape of the Church. It will, for example, mean that the Church will have to face up to being thrust into the centre of the realities of life in ways sensitive to the most vulnerable members of society.

What will this mean for the practice of the Church, and what will it say to those in society concerned with the poor? To put these questions together reveals a belief about God, society and the relationship between them which suggests ways to answer them. If Christian belief and discipleship are concerned with the realities of life as revealed by analysis and related practice, then those realities are invested with a supreme significance for Christians. To make this discovery has major implications for society as well as the Churches.

For society it means that because these realities are taken seriously by Christians, then whatever thought and practice emerges from involvement with them could be of as much value to society as to the Churches. For the Churches it means that it is in the midst of these realities that God is to be found and served. To address them in this belief must therefore become an integral part of what Christianity and Church life is all about. It will mean the Church learning to take seriously in its relationship to society and in its attitude to its own life what careful analysis and related policies in the poverty field reveal. Consistency alone will require that the rejection of an undue emphasis on the individualist explanations of poverty and the defective policies associated with them will need to be accompanied by the Church freeing itself from its domination by a profound and all-pervasive individualism.

Yet for the good of the Church and of society it is important to do more than chart out the religious complement to the three main responses to poverty already identified. The need to move beyond these more traditional responses has already been noted. The forces of industrial change and the need to remove poverty from society clearly compel the formulation of new practices.

How can this be done? It may be possible, by addressing what poverty should mean for the practice of the Church, to move beyond the limitations of the traditional responses. Such new ways of involvement by the Church could well contain valuable lessons for society because they face up to individualism through the challenge of caring, face up to localities through the challenge of involvement in community, and face up to structures through the challenge of social vision and the forming of pressure groups in the Church.

1. FACING UP TO INDIVIDUALISM: THE CHALLENGE OF CARING.

Christians and the Church have always responded positively to poverty by practical caring, and the last two centuries have proved to be no exception to this tradition. The growth of dire poverty in nineteenth century towns and cities was complemented by a vast demonstration of private and public charity. Even in 1850 London charities had an annual income of £2½ million, and in the next ten years 144 new charitable institutions were founded in the capital. Varying from simple good neighbourly help to the clinical case-work approach of the Charity Organisation Society, all were concerned to alleviate the desperate condition of the poor. Indeed, the Settlement Movement actually colonised the East Ends of our cities with great buildings from which Oxbridge graduates attempted to meet the physical, educational and leisure needs of the poor.

Although the forms may sometimes have changed, such practical caring continues to dominate the Church's response to poverty in the 1980s. Good neighbour schemes, counselling and drop-in centres for the unemployed, old folk's lunch clubs, youth clubs, and jumble sales often reveal the all-pervasive influence of the philanthropic response to human need.

Yet important as is this practical Christian involvement with the poor, it has to be strongly questioned in the light of the explanations of poverty which have begun to emerge. These have shown how the predicament of the poor cannot be accounted for satisfactorily by reference to their personal defects. If the poor are rather victims of social forces, then policies which blame them for their plight or seek to educate and train them out of their defects can never be an adequate response to their problems. This analysis and judgment applies equally to the Church's emphasis on practical caring schemes catering for the problems of individual poor people. Their concern to work with the symptoms of social malaise draws attention away from and therefore gives support to the causes of that malaise. In Tawney's splendid comment: 'They seem to be alleviating distress while they really are the embodiment of the principles by which distress is produced'. These words should be written into every ordination charge, every Board of Social Responsibility constitution and every annual congregational review.

The pursuit of justice for the poor rules out much of the Church's traditional practical caring work as an inadequate engagement with the issue of poverty, because it is done for inaccurate reasons (like remedying the defects of the poor) and therefore done in the wrong way. Yet practical caring can never be condemned as such. To care for those less able to help themselves is a primary Christian obligation. Where humanity is at its most vulnerable amongst the poor, the children, the sick and the aged, there God is to be particularly sought, worshipped and served. The question to be faced is therefore not whether Christians should care but for what reasons and in what ways. Is there a way of caring which takes account of the responsibility to care for others and the implications for caring of an adequate analysis of poverty? Such a way has begun to emerge through our understanding of the poor which suggests new reasons for caring and new ways of caring.

Why should we care? If you look at defective caring policies you will often see that their weaknesses spring from defective motivations. If one of our concerns is to care for others in the most adequate way open to us, then what can we learn from such defective motivations? There are three negative lessons:

We should not care in order to improve the moral or religious character of the recipient.

We should not care in order to satisfy our own psychological needs (the alleviation of guilt).

We should not care in order to avoid social upheaval or revolution.

If these are the ways we should not care, then how should we care? There are three good reasons for caring:

We should care because we are asserting the supreme importance of what it means to be a human being. To care is to help others to become more fulfilled.

We should care because we too have to grow. Helping others to grow to their fulfilment is to help us to grow to our fulfilment. There is a profound mutuality in living and caring, since if one is diminished all are diminished.

We should care because to promote an understanding of what it means to be fully human is in itself a contribution to a better understanding of God. It is to serve God and to expedite the coming of his Kingdom.

How should we care? Motivations for concern always lead into ways for working them out in practice. There are two classic ways in which caring is expressed in our society. First, there are those who choose to use their resources to do things *for* and *to* people. A large number of charismatic community workers, including clergymen, use their skills to attract often considerable funding and other resources for their particular project or community often at the expense of more important needs. Many local schemes have also received funds from the Manpower Services Commission to employ full-time help from amongst the unemployed only to see a marked decline in volunteer and part-time effort. In both examples, work done for people and communities has harmed the voluntary work done by people and communities.

Secondly, there are those who use their resources to do things *with* rather than *for* people, so that men and women learn to develop their own lives, communities and associations in their own ways. So much of this kind of caring is essentially about promoting that voluntary effort which avoids the pitfalls of philanthropy by helping the more powerless members of our society to gain a greater say over it and their own lives.

Given growing poverty, to develop good motives for caring for the poor and good ways of caring with the poor is to begin to rehabilitate the noble virtue of philanthropy. By facing the question of poverty in these ways we are driven not to make the poor like us but rather to enter a process of change which will affect us as much as them. Since one of the great troubles with poverty and charity is that they divide the affluent from the poor, any process which promotes mutual understanding and benefit is to be welcomed. Indeed, unless defective and hostile attitudes to the poor and the deferential postures often shown by the poor to their supposed superiors are radically amended, there will be no successful and long-term erosion of poverty. Involvement with the poor frees the Church to define and promote with a new confidence and relevance what it means to care and be pastoral. It equally re-establishes the obligation and opportunity for individuals to care in an increasingly institutionalized society.

2. Facing up to Localities: the Challenge of Involvement in Community.

There is a strength and inevitability about the domination of the Church's involvement in society by area-based responses. More than any other organization it has maintained its presence in local communities. Indeed, the extent, quality and continuity of the support given to its activities by its members far outweighs that of any other political, industrial or leisure organization. Given its commitment to people, this involvement with people where they actually are in their localities is not surprising. This area-based involvement has taken two main forms which in turn have shaped the Church's engagement with the issue of poverty.

The first, and by far the biggest activity, is the community or parochial model which is symbolized by the presence of the church building and minister in a neighbourhood. The second, the chaplaincy model, is represented by the presence of a minister within an institution like a hospital, prison, university, or factory. Although often seen as the opposing models of parochial versus specialist ministries, in practice they operate essentially in similar ways within specific geographical areas.

Despite the strength and inevitability of such locality-based involvement in society, it must be seen to suffer from the same kind of defects as the area response to poverty. Both relate to people where they are, whether at home, at work or in hospital. Yet both as a result fail to engage those social forces which so shape the lives of men and women and which so often lie beyond local boundaries. Major decisions about housing, redundancies, health care and prison populations are not made where people live and work, or where they are nursed or incarcerated. Consequently, the poverty of the poor cannot be explained or combatted by ministries which relate to either the personal problems of the poor or their communities, whether where they live or where they work.

If the Church's area-based involvement in society is so organized as to make it incapable of adequately engaging these forces which shape the lives of men and women, then in what ways can it begin to address those forces more effectively? How can it move beyond local boundaries but yet in such a way as to feed back into the local, because that is where people are and therefore where policies must be judged?

Faced with the reality of poverty and with the defects of the area response to it, there are three ways in which the locality can be transcended for the benefit of the locality. Related as they are to the Church's attempt to combat poverty they have implications for both the Church's involvement in other issues and for secular social policies in general.

The first is *the importance of properly recognizing the community as local* by working through it in ways which take account of the forces beyond it. Although many now see that the causes of deindustrialization and unemployment lie outside local communities this has often led them to desert the local for a more amorphous project work with issues and organizations. Lacking roots in localities such work has often become as unaccountable and indefinable as the forces it presumes to engage. The defects of the area response have been replaced by different defects without maintaining the virtues of local work.

How can the local community be properly recognized in ways which acknowledge the influence of forces beyond it, and yet allow local people to have a stake in it? To do this requires selecting a representative entry point into what is shaping community life, for example unemployment, and then developing two policies. On the one hand, it involves bringing people from local churches together to discover the nature, extent and causes of unemployment in their area and beyond. On the other hand, it then involves building practical projects in the light of their analysis of unemployment. This would mean, for example, designing projects with the unemployed following three guidelines: *to whom* are the projects addressed (those like the unskilled and under-24s who bear the biggest burden of unemployment), *with whom* are they being done (the unemployed, local community groups, trade unions, employers, and local authorities), and *what longer-term goals* are they seeking to move towards (what are the real needs of local communities, what kind of permanent employment are they seeking to create, and how will people have a say in them)?

The second way in which the locality can be transcended is through *the importance of properly recognizing the community as part of the wider society* by working at different levels in ways which acknowledge their distinctive contribution to each other. So often, the churches at the local level are highly critical of diocesan or regional and nationally-based Church organizations, and so often the latter conduct their affairs apart from local needs. Faced with issues like poverty the Church has little choice but to find ways of developing strategies to which *the different levels* can clearly contribute from their distinctive experiences and positions. Equally, because it is by what is happening to people where they are that it will be judged, it has to discover ways of both resourcing local involvement from diocesan and national levels, and influencing the practices of the latter by reference to the realities and needs of the poor in their communities. This would mean, for example, that industrial mission and community work would become integral parts of the Church's involvement with people in their places of employment and in their local communities. They would not be a specialist function doing such work on behalf of, and often quite separate from, the Church and its members. They would be so re-formed that they would resource Church involvement with issues like poverty and deindustrialization. Equally, the ministry based in parish or local community would be encouraged to relate to such strategies because it would no longer be operating from an essentially defective and limited view of the locality.

Third, comes *the importance of properly recognising the community as more than the neighbourhood* by taking account of the needs and resources of people in the different sectors of their life in urban society. If the unskilled worker's poverty is caused significantly by the low wages he receives at work, the Church's involvement with that cannot be properly separated from its involvement with him in his bad housing and in his children's poor school and health. The Church's poverty strategies have to find ways of working across these sectors, and therefore across the parochial and chaplaincy ministries, across the different Church departments like education, social responsibility, industrial mission and community work.

Poverty demands, but also offers the opportunity for, all these responses which more adequately face up to what it means to be properly involved in community.

3. Facing up to Structures: Beyond Politics, the Challenge of Social Vision, and the Emergence of a Pressure Group in the Church.

To be immersed in the problem of poverty and then to struggle with what can be done about it is to enter invariably into the realms of political life. All the explanations of poverty and the policies associated with them, contain a powerful political dimension. Whether considering the role of institutions or class, or recognizing far-reaching questions about work, income and social tissue, all require taking politics seriously. Yet although such a conclusion is right, one feels more and more that the answer is somehow wrong. The forces of industrial change are now so radical in their effects that traditional political life is patently unable openly to face up to the questions they raise or to find credible answers to them. Indeed, the very mention of the word 'politics' at this stage of an argument is guaranteed to produce at best an anti-climax and at worse cynicism or downright hostility. How can one face up to what taking poverty seriously requires of people, whilst avoiding the deadly pitfalls associated with the practice of politics? In what ways can the Church, in its involvement with the poor, be politically more than political? To begin to find answers to these questions is of importance to both Church and society. Indeed, unless answers are found, poverty will flourish and the hope of a more caring Church and society will never be realized.

Beyond Politics: The Pursuit of Collective Action.
The problem of politics being at a low ebb is compounded by the traditional Christian rejection of political involvement as part of Church life and witness. A recent survey of Anglican General Synod members revealed that few had

interests outside the Church, with only 12 per cent showing concern about social and political problems. Yet an understanding of the structures of society is vital for a proper grasp of the causes of poverty and what can be done about it. If people in general and Church members in particular therefore seek to make an effective impact on the persistence of poverty they will have to move beyond the current misunderstanding and rejection of politics in order to work on what are essentially political matters.

How can this be done? What the predicament of the poor has taught us offers a way forward if it is used to put flesh on Tawney's definition of politics. He described it as 'the art of achieving by collective actions ends which cannot be attained with the same measure of success by individuals acting in isolation'. What has been recognized about the importance of income and relationships for human fulfilment clearly suggests the need to obtain adequate resources for people. However, it also suggests, given the significance of relationships for people, the appropriateness of collective activity as a means for achieving such a goal. Politics understood through these categories can therefore be seen to reflect and promote the essential humanity of men and women. It offers a means of asserting once again the importance of politics for people and therefore for Christians because both are passionately committed to defending and enhancing what it means to be human.

It is worth pausing to reflect on the significance of this conclusion. It does not simply assert the importance of politics for the very being of men and women. It also recognizes the possibility open to people of changing their society in accordance with their beliefs. Both are the two sides of the one coin about people, both are essential for effective facing up to poverty. Indeed, together they challenge current orthodoxies about basic humanity as promoted by theologians like Dr E.R. Norman and by politicians like Mrs Thatcher. In his Reith lectures, the former declared, 'I do not believe in the natural goodness of man ... I think on the whole people are rubbish and they deserve to be awakened to the need to change and amend themselves, not by some social factor or by some force of circumstance, but by conversion of their soul'. Mrs Thatcher, on her part, preaches a belief in the mechanism of the market which people, if they have any sense, will accept and complement by changing what they can change, which is their attitudes. Both theologian and politician betray a lack of conviction that people through politics are capable of changing for the better not simply themselves but also their environment, including the market place.

The understanding of the essential humanity of people emerging from a study of poverty suggests a very different view of people. It suggests that the structural problems associated with rapid industrial change and the persistence of poverty can be faced with real possibilities of improvement in the direction of greater justice and community, and that the structures of society are not fixed and unalterable but are susceptible of modification. The existence of sin forbids unqualified optimism, but the grace of God requires people not only to have hopes but to work for expressions of them which are feasible in the here and now.

With such an understanding of politics as collective action, what does it mean for the Church to engage in it? Since people are being pressed to move beyond old understandings and practices, traditional exhortations alone cannot be repeated. It can no longer be sufficient to urge Christians to get involved in political parties and trade union branches. That is to encourage men and women to become involved in part of the cause of the problem they are seeking to address. Instead, the understanding of what Christians can do about collective action should move them to develop social vision and encourage the emergence of pressure groups. With such a critical apparatus they can then play a discerning part in the traditional politics of government and industry because they will be seeking to move beyond them for the sake of the poor and our common humanity.

Social Vision: the Challenge to and from the Church.
To be involved effectively in society over an issue like poverty requires more than collective action. It demands a view of the goals towards which one is seeking to move. It requires a vision of the kind of society desired beyond the disappearance of poverty.

In the light of the above conclusions about poverty and the need to move beyond old understandings, what kind of society should Christians aim for? It is doubtful whether the answer is to promote a Christian theory of society as though there is a view of society peculiar to Christians. This would go against the Christian recognition of the supreme importance of men and women and of human society. Yet the implications of this understanding of poverty and Christianity for what it means to be human suggest, for people in general and certainly for Christians in particular, hard tests of the moral adequacy of a society or social policy. The Church may not be able to achieve any real consensus over particular policies to be pursued in economic or social affairs. It may well be inappropriate for it to come up with alternative economic strategies to the ones being currently pursued. But what it can and must do is to speak out in a decisive and clear way when certain agreed values about our basic humanity become clearly endangered. It must say that, whatever the policy may be, the costs to be paid by ordinary men and women are unacceptable.

There are five tests of particular policies and the view of society they represent which are suggested by a consideration of poverty. Each seeks to move beyond the old understandings, and each has direct implications for Church policies.

First, in what ways and to what extent do policies care for those least able to help themselves? Do they positively assist or indeed discriminate in favour of children, the elderly, the sick, the handicapped, those in prison, the poor? By framing the test so that it includes other vulnerable groups besides the poor any negative responses associated with an undue emphasis on the poor can be avoided. It clearly

112

derives from the Judaeo-Christian tradition, yet also appeals to all who are concerned to promote a more morally adequate society.

The implications of this test for the Church's own life are profound and numerous and include a radical questioning of its use of resources. These are traditionally and increasingly concentrated in relation to the more advantaged areas and classes as the withdrawal from the inner cities proceeds apace.

Secondly, in what ways and to what extent do policies reduce those divisions in society which separate people and communities from each other and generate attitudes of superiority and deference? Do they remove the barriers between us and them and promote a growing awareness of what people hold in common as human beings? To put the test in this way avoids the divisiveness associated with people's understanding of equality. It requires the Church to erode the harmful separation of clergy from laity and men from women which is so wasteful of human resources and potential.

Thirdly, in what ways and to what extent do policies encourage people to have more and more say over matters which affect their daily lives and the life of society? This test moves far beyond the increasingly tired concept of participation and if applied to the Church would dramatically affect its whole social balance. It would mean, on the one hand, insisting on at least the proportionate involvement of the unskilled and semi-skilled on decision-making bodies of all kinds and at all levels, from local and national synods to specialist boards and councils. (One can only view with the gravest alarm the recent survey of the General Synod of the Church of England which revealed that 96 per cent of the lay members interviewed were upper middle-class by occupation compared with 1 per cent working-class. As a 'Guardian' report further commented, 'even within such an unrepresentative Synod there was an inner élite increasingly holding the power for policy making' further disadvantaging the already disadvantaged). Such a proposed discrimination in favour of the working classes would clearly need to be accompanied by training such members for leadership in ways respecting their experiences and skills. It would also mean deliberately fostering the involvement of churches with working-class communities, cultures and organizations.

Fourthly, in what ways and to what extent do policies encourage a view of society operating as society, not just as a bulwark against wrongdoing but also as a promoter of good relationships? Even in the nineteenth century, for example, with reference to the employment of children in factories, society recognized that, wherever 'the rights of property became the wrongs of the poor, then there was a case for intervention to create the very conditions in which mutual self-help and competition could freely operate'. Since then, many have come to see that the benefits to be gained by the poor from education will be minimal unless accompanied by significant improvements in the housing, health and income levels of the poor. Avoiding unhelpful conflicts over strong or weak views of the State, this test also raises important questions for the Church in its relationships with the State. Should a major Church like the Church of England or the Church of Scotland be established and therefore enmeshed with the very forces, classes and institutions which are a major cause of the existence and persistence of large-scale poverty? Should the Church as a voluntary body continue the British tradition of pioneering work in education, health and personal caring and then handing it over to the State and therefore out of the reach of the influence of ordinary people? Is this not precisely what voluntary bodies, or 'intermediate associations' as William Temple called them, exist to prevent? (By this he meant bodies which stand between the individual and the State and are therefore more accessible to the influence of the individual and can protect him from the State). Has the time not come for a major rethink of the relationship between the State and the voluntary sector in general and the Church in particular? The Church's vocation to care for those less able to help themselves will inevitably require a critical distancing from the State and the established orderings of society. What will this mean for the Christendom tradition of the Church's partnership with the State?

Fifthly, in what ways and to what extent do policies promote the viability of society and the communities within it? Without economic viability the pursuit of justice in a modern urban society becomes a dispensable luxury. There is no sense in pursuing the redistribution of wealth if all become poor, and there is no hope for the poor if viability is not pursued in ways strongly sensitive to the other four tests of policy. By moving beyond the hang-ups associated with the profit-motive, the test of social viability asks of the Church a number of responses. It encourages it to advocate the proper and efficient social costing of all decisions affecting people and therefore to test them by what they actually do to people, and especially the more vulnerable members of society. (What is the true cost of deflationary monetarist policies or of traditional collectivization programmes?) It also gives the Church the responsibility to support wealth-creating industries through its national investment policies and to find ways of encouraging local employment-creating initiatives through its community-based churches.

Important as are these five tests of the moral adequacy of a society or policy, for either to pass them successfully would not mean that such a society was the Kingdom of God. Yet the Kingdom of God can never be anything less than what these tests suggest about life. As moral impact statements they are what social vision needs to take seriously, because they arise out of a proper consideration of what it means to be poor in today's society.

The Emergence of a Pressure Group in the Church.

If the Church is to do anything about poverty it has at least to ask radical questions about the way society is structured. Yet it has to do more than this. It also has to take its questions into the field of political decision-making. Official Church bodies of the denominational or ecumenical type are rarely able to do the former. Their tradition has been to produce eminently sensible consensus reports on social matters whose very balance means they avoid asking any radical questions. They are inevitably located within those established orderings of society which are part of the cause of poverty. They are therefore rarely able to translate social criticisms into political realities with any degree of commitment, coherence or continuity. Yet the implications of poverty and Christianity for our understanding of people and what must be done to enhance their lives suggest that this is precisely what some Church bodies must do. Promoting collective action sensitive to the plight of the poor has to work out social vision in the particulars of society. That is what the practice of going beyond politics in response to poverty requires of the Church.

Given that the five tests begin to offer a way of making sense of social vision, how can the Church appropriately and realistically pursue the demands of such vision within the political arena? It was in answer to that key question that some Christians, after a number of years spent struggling with poverty, began to test out the feasibility of operating as a pressure group within the Church around the issue of poverty. As a result of their discussions Church Action on Poverty was formed in 1982. Although separate from official Church bodies like denominational social responsibility boards and the British Council of Churches (yet relating to them where it was felt to be mutually useful), they sought to avoid becoming a sectarian group since they hoped to influence as many Church bodies and Christians as possible. In other words, they rejected becoming either part of that establishment which is a cause of poverty or a splinter group condemned to irrelevance because of its political unrealism. Taking the Church seriously has never meant, of course, that relationships would not be developed with bodies like the Child Poverty Action Group who have a similar concern for the poor. That kind of isolationism would contradict their commitment to an essential humanity shared by all men and women.

What is the value of such a pressure group? First and foremost it offers an opportunity to bring people and groups together across the lines of party (both political and theological), social class and department (for example, parochial ministry, industrial mission and community work) to pursue an issue of vital concern for the health of society. Secondly, it allows the Church to develop a political voice in ways which are appropriate to the Church and yet politically realistic. By an appropriate political voice is meant avoiding motions placed before Church assemblies which are either so politically divisive as to be counterproductive, or so general as to mean anything to anybody. Church Action on Poverty plans to do this by selecting particular political issues and policies which are seen to clearly represent the Church's understanding of God and his commitment to humanity. For example, such an issue is the determination to increase benefits for the long-term unemployed by putting them onto the long-term supplementary benefit scale like every other group dependent on social security. If those without work for over twelve months are the victims of industrial change then they must be protected like the elderly and sick, from poverty. Since this is such a controversial area, many like William Temple would say that the Church should not be politically involved in this way. Yet the Church can act in a politically authentic way without being politically offensive to parties because it has carefully asked itself why it is involved, for whom and in what way, and then acted openly on this basis. By politically realistic, is meant the setting of objectives achievable by the classic methods used by pressure groups. These include good organization, the careful marshalling of evidence, public meetings, pamphlets, petitions and lobbying. Given the great achievements of pressure groups in the nineteenth century in their campaigns for a better society 'there is no reason to put any a priori limit to the efficiency of this pressure'.

What will such a pressure group do? It will seek to bring together Christians and Church bodies on the basis of a general agreement over definitions and explanations of poverty and a general determination to do something about it. By selecting particular objectives which represented some of the key realities of poverty (like, for example, raising the long-term unemployed and child benefit rates, developing fair housing subsidies, and attacking low pay), it will promote their discussion and acceptance through all the appropriate levels and departments of the Church's life. In this way both the individual and corporate aspects of Christian life should become familiar with the realities of poverty. On the basis of such attitude-changing Church life could be transformed and its political voice used to influence for the good the life of society in general and then government policies in particular.

Concern for the poor has driven us to consider the structures of society. That consideration has inevitably meant taking collective action seriously to try to make visions for society work. Such a struggle is both profoundly human and profoundly Christian. Yet ways have always to be found to express it within the actual particulars of the political life of the Church and of society. The idea of a pressure group concerned with poverty is only one such means, but it could offer a way of making social visions viable. Tawney noted the importance of attempting this when he wrote how 'someone has written on the long dreams of youth; but, in my experience, unless they are shown to be at least partly realisable in the not too-distant future, the life of such visions is sure to be short'. That cannot be allowed to happen: the poor are too important for everyone. A pressure group could administer 'the tonic required to turn discontent and aspirations into convictions'. An agenda for action is emerging. Church Action on Poverty could be an instrument for putting that agenda into practice.

Resources for Involvement: What the Poor Mean for a Way of Life

If asked what are the most important lessons to be learned from an enquiry into poverty it should be said, without hesitation, discovering what it means to be human and how to face issues like poverty. Beyond any reasonable doubt the poor demonstrate that material resources and freedom in relationships are absolutely essential for any human living with any hope of fulfilment. Contrasting the actual lives of Mary, Mike, Ann, Jim, Barbara, Dave, Mr and Mrs Brown, and their children, with what so many wrongly feel about the poor, should drive people to analyse the predicament of the poor and then to do something about it.

Despite the value of these conclusions there are at least two further matters to be considered which are central to any adequate engagement with poverty. They arise out of the recognition that the power of industrial change and the apparent intractability of poverty produce the uneasy conviction that 'all has not been said which must be said'. Of equal importance to Church and society, even though more obviously concerned with the former, these two matters can be described as how life is approached and how life is lived. (These phrases are preferred to the traditional concepts of theology and spirituality because the need to move beyond old ways of doing things is nowhere more required than in Church thought and practice).

How life is approached. There has always been a deep division between thought and practice which has invariably been to the detriment of the quality of life in general and to the plight of the poor in particular. Within a complex urban-industrial society the effects of that departmentalizing of key aspects of human living become even more damaging. It means that governments still pursue policies which ignore what all major studies of poverty have revealed for generations. The whole of institutional life is still powerfully impregnated with the inaccurate view that the poor are poor because it's their own fault. It means too, that thinking in its academic form is normally pursued in ways quite divorced from what goes on in the everyday life of society. Too often books on educational theory use language and ideas which bear little resemblance to the daily struggle of teachers to survive in inner city classrooms. A world-famous theologian can give a powerful lecture on Christ the expiatory sacrifice which bears no sign of being delivered in Manchester in the last decades of the twentieth century; it could just as easily have been delivered in third century Antioch.

There is surely something profoundly and indeed inherently wrong with a way of approaching life which so fragments human experience. There is a growing feeling among many people that it is the way in which life is approached, by holding together within a durable partnership rigorous analysis and purposeful practice, which holds the way forward for human living. (One says 'rigorous' analysis because so often attendance at lectures or seminars by clergy or laity is marked by their failure to bring with them pen and paper. Sometimes there is nothing more impractical than so-called practical people). The placing of the emphasis in that partnership will depend on whether a contribution should be seen as essentially more theoretical or more practical. Yet both operate within the framework of the partnership. Both begin, from the Christian's point of view, by addressing the realities of life as a human being who is a Christian. The development from that base in a reflective way is what theology must be about. The development from that base in a practical way is what practice must be about. Each can only develop by learning from the other in relation to the same realities. Both can be a dialogue with the essential humanity of people because what God has done in Christ through the Incarnation means that the dialogue with the human can become a dialogue with God. That is why this book, in terms of what it has tackled, how it has tackled it, and why it has tackled it, can be seen to be an essentially theological exercise. It is as though social surveys and government white papers on the human predicament become the proper source material for the development of contemporary theology, profoundly affecting its very shape, content and language.

Many people are being driven to the conclusion that, unless thought and practice become one in all their doing and thinking, they will never approach their fulfilment as human beings. Without this partnership as one flesh, what causes poverty will never be removed from society. If that is so for human living it is doubly so for Christian thought and practice. For Christian thought it surely means that it must always clearly bear the signs of the times in which it lives. Once again it would then be able to play a full and proper part in the conversations of the market place. For Christian practice it means, for example, that even Church architecture will not simply reflect current trends but will also comment upon them out of its beliefs about people.

Of course, to be so in touch with the realities of poverty and urban life will inevitably transform the shape of existing Christian thought and practice. It will invariably mean that Christians are put at a distance from their previous self-understandings of faith, theology and discipleship. Yet, if 'the future wears an ominous visage for all who want to apply old remedies to new ailments', what other option could a hopeful and realistic way of life entail?

How life is lived. Even if thinking and practising is based on the same facing up to realities it will not be sufficient to cope with what society is now demanding of people. What has to be taught and what has to be practised, in the face of the persistence of poverty, can only be carried through to successful conclusions if it is translated into the actual lives of individuals, groups and organizations. It will only permeate the realities of life because it is actually lived by men and women, and by Christians especially. The sad divisions between thought and practice are nowhere more harmful in their effects than when people do not live lives compatible with their beliefs. Whether considering those who proclaim concern for the poor and yet pay for their children to be privately educated, or whether considering a Church which says it is concerned for the most vulnerable in society and yet draws only 1 per cent of its governing body from the working classes, a damaging inconsistency emerges which is destructive of the credibility required for any successful pursuit of justice.

The theologian Karl Barth rightly rejected the liberal theology of his youth when he discovered that his teachers had signed a letter supporting the Kaiser's invasion of Belgium in 1914. If that was what their theology led them to do, then for Barth their theology must be wrong. Theology could never be separated from a way of life. The former was tested by the latter in the light of whether it was productive of justice.

What, then, does an understanding of poverty mean for a way of life? It will mean taking seriously analyses and practices suggested by an adequate study of poverty, so that the truth about poverty is vigilantly promoted wherever false attitudes and perceptions exist, whether in our own lives or in the communal life of the organizations with which we are involved.

Secondly, because of an understanding of what it means to be human, such a view of poverty will encourage good and effective relationships between people, groups, organizations and levels of society. Inevitably this will mean promoting mutual decision-making and accountability within the family, between minister, congregation and community, and between the different levels of the Church's life.

Thirdly, and again deriving from an understanding of what it means to be human, it will mean developing an attitude to resources which will inevitably lead to a greater simplicity of life for the more affluent as they diminish their hold on resources in order to allow the disadvantaged to increase theirs. It could mean the emergence of a new and more generous puritanism full of simplicity, humility and daily service in communities of all kinds.

Fourthly, it will demand a clarity of vision and a toughness of purpose, since all these practices and understandings will be vigorously or subtly resisted by individual and corporate selfishness and sin, including our own. In other words, the calling to be fully human will demand from each person a form of discipleship which taking the poor seriously graciously reveals.

The 1980s will be a most disturbing decade. As Britain's decline relative to other leading nations continues, the grave weaknesses in her social systems and way of life will become more and more apparent. Sadly, there is every possibility that the growing number of poor will pay the heaviest price for that decline and for those weaknesses. What a study of the poor reveals must not simply be taken seriously by society and the Church, but must be done so with great urgency. The time may well be very short before the divisions in society will become so bad that a body like the Church, as in South America, will be compelled to declare whose side it is on. The signs of such an approaching time for decision have been seen in the furore over the Church's decision to make grants to the Liverpool 8 Defence Committee. Normally the Church at large has assumed that it can pick and choose which signs to take notice of. That is to miss the whole point of the

123

nature and significance of the signs of the times. They always communicate a reality which will act as a judgment upon people if they do not take it most seriously. It is precisely through this reality that the truths of the Christian understanding of the human have to be proclaimed. What is happening to the poor may well be such a sign offered to the emerging Church.

The intention throughout these pages has been to see what poverty really is and what it drives us to do, in the firm belief that this is a way in which God is to be found, worshipped and served. To build an emerging Church on that belief would be of value to all men and women even if poverty was not banished from society as Lloyd George hoped. The understanding of what it means to be human which that belief would proclaim would far outweigh the inevitable failings and shortcomings of people and institutions. A society which 'is convinced that inequality is an evil need not be alarmed because the evil is one which cannot wholly be subdued. In recognizing the poison it will have armed itself with an antidote. It will have deprived inequality of its sting by stripping it of its esteem'. It may be possible to see no further than this, but maybe that is sufficient this side of heaven.

REFERENCES AND FURTHER READING

For those who wish to take further points made in the previous pages and read other books on poverty, the following references and suggestions for reading should be helpful. They are not meant to be exhaustive, but should enable readers to pursue their particular interests in more detail. Of the newly published books the following are particularly useful and are not found in the references:

David Donnison: *The Politics of Poverty*, Martin Robertson, 1982.
    An inside view of government policy-making by the last Chairman of the Supplementary Benefits Commission.
Susanne MacGregor, *The Politics of Poverty*, Longman, 1981. A survey of modern poverty in the political scene.
Julian Le Grand, *The Strategy of Equality, Redistribution and the Social Services*, Allen and Unwin, 1982.
Louie Burghes and Ruth Lister (eds), *Unemployment: Who Pays the Price?* Poverty Pamphlet 53, CPAG, 1981.
David Piachaud, *Children and Poverty*, Poverty Research Series 9, CPAG, 1981.

INTRODUCTION

page 1.   David Lloyd George, Hansard, 29 April 1909. Quoted in *The Evolution of the British Welfare State*, Derek Fraser, Macmillan, 1973, (pp. 145–6). A most useful historical survey.

125

page 2.   Andrew Mearns, *The Bitter Cry of Outcast London*, (1883). This, along with excerpts from other classic studies of poverty (including Booth and Rowntree), can be found in *Into Unknown England, 1866–1913*, edited by Peter Keating, Fontana-Collins, 1976, p. 91. (The emphasis in the quotation is mine).

CHAPTER ONE

page 5.   Quoted in Robert Holman, *Poverty*, Martin Robertson, 1978, p. 46. One of the best surveys of poverty, which particularly examines the different explanations of poverty.

Ronald Gregor Smith, *The Free Man*, Collins, 1969, p. 36.

The Four Experiences of Poverty (pp. 6–16) are drawn from a variety of sources including:

(a)   Jean Coussins and Anna Coote, *The Family in the Firing Line*, Poverty Pamphlet 51, March 1981. (Published by the Child Poverty Action Group, CPAG, 1 Macklin Street, London WC2B 5NH. This is the main pressure group in the poverty field, and its regular publications are excellent value).

(b)   Louie Burghes, *Living from Hand to Mouth*, Pamphlet 50, December 1980, joint FSU-CPAG publication. Important study of 65 families living on Supplementary Benefit.

(c)   Peter Townsend, *Poverty in the United Kingdom*, Penguin, 1979 (see especially Chapter Nine). A magisterial survey of the whole poverty issue. Despite its size, each chapter is a manageable unit, with a brief introduction and conclusion.

(d)   Frank Coffield, Philip Robinson, Jacquie Sarsby, *A Cycle of Deprivation*, Heinemann Educational Books, 1980. Detailed case studies of four families.

Statistics. These are drawn from a variety of sources including *Social Trends*, HMSO, published annually; Supplementary Benefit Commission *Annual Reports*; the *Department of Employment Gazette* (published monthly, giving detailed breakdown of unemployment figures, etc); the *General Household Survey* (HMSO, published annually); and the books noted above, especially Holman, Townsend, Coussins and Coote.

The Affluent (pp. 16–18): Two main sources:

(a) *The Wealth Report*, edited by Frank Field, Routledge & Kegan Paul, 1979.

(b) Peter Townsend (as above), Chapter Nine (for the accounts of Mr and Mrs Margood, and Mr and Mrs Avis-Brown).

page 18. Benjamin Disraeli, *Sybil*, Penguin, 1980, p. 96. Nineteenth century novels are a most illuminating source of concepts used in the present understanding of poverty.

CHAPTER TWO

page 19. The account of Mr Dibshoss is found in Peter Townsend's study, p. 353.

page 19F. Material on perceptions and attitudes to poverty can be found in Peter Golding, *Poverty—What Poverty*? in Poverty No.44, December 1979—the journal of the CPAG. This edition contains in addition useful surveys of Peter Townsend's book. Also see Peter Townsend, Chapter Eleven.

page 22. The EEC survey refers to *The Perception of Poverty in Europe*, Commission of the European Communities, 1977.

page 23. Sources for the discussion of income and wealth distribution can be found in the *Reports of the Royal Commission on the Distribution of Income and Wealth*, (HMSO), in the *Wealth Report* (above), and in Peter Townsend (above).

page 26. R.H. Tawney, *Religion and the Rise of Capitalism*, Murray, 1926, p. 268.

page 27. R.H. Tawney, *Equality*, Allen and Unwin, (4th ed. 1952). These two books by Tawney are among the classics of history and social thought.

page 28. *The Humanity of God* is explored in a book of that title by Karl Barth, Fontana-Collins.
page 29. Quoted in Holman, (above) p. 252.

CHAPTER THREE

page 34. The cartoon can be found in the Easter, 1981, edition of *The Coracle*, the newspaper of the Iona Community.
page 35. R.H. Tawney, *Equality*, preface.
page 36. Booth and Rowntree's classic definitions of poverty can be found in Keating's *Into Unknown England*, (above), p. 113 and p. 194.
page 37. *Supplementary Benefits Commission, Annual Report 1978*, HMSO, 1979, paras. 1.3 and 1.4. The SBC has now been replaced by the Social Security Advisory Committee.
pages 37–8. Useful discussions of supplementary benefit levels and poverty can be found in Holman (above) and Frank Field, *Inequality in Britain: Freedom, Welfare and the State*, Fontana, 1981. The latter contains much useful information on the whole poverty issue.
pages 40–2. For definitions of relative deprivation—see Townsend (above), pp. 31,88. Linda Chalker's comments as Under Secretary of State at the DHSS can be found in *Living from Hand to Mouth*, (above).
page 43. Professor Donnison's observations are made in *Poverty*, no. 44 (above).
pages 44–7. Groups particularly affected by poverty—statistics can be found in Holman and Townsend (above).
page 48. R.H. Tawney, *Poverty as an Industrial Problem*, in *R.H. Tawney: The American Labour Movement and Other Essays*, Harvester Press, 1979.
pages 49–50. Statistics on the distribution of income and wealth can be found in Townsend, Holman, Frank Field, and *The Wealth Report* (above).
page 49. Malcolm Dean, *The Guardian*, 28 January 1980.

CHAPTER FOUR

page 52.   Tawney, *Equality*, preface.

page 53F.   Useful examinations of the explanations of poverty will be found in Holman and Townsend (above), but especially in the former from whom most of the references in this chapter are drawn unless otherwise stated.

pages 57–8.   *R.H. Tawney's Commonplace Book*, (ed) J.M. Winter and D.M. Joslin, Cambridge University Press, 1972.

C. Wright Mills, *The Sociological Imagination*, Penguin, 1970, p. 15.

pages 58–9.   On class, see Holman (above).

pages 59–60.   Élites—see *An Anatomy of the British Ruling Class*, Anthony Giddens, in *New Society*, 4 October 1979, and *Origins and Destinations, Family Class and Education in Modern Britain*, A.H. Halsey, A.F. Heath, and J.M. Ridge, Clarendon Press, 1980. A more accessible version of Halsey's views will be found in his *Change in British Society*, Oxford University Press, 1978.

pages 61–3.   On the Welfare State in general, and the four additional 'welfare states', see F. Field, *Inequality in Britain*, (above).

page 63.   Holman (above), p. 181.

CHAPTER FIVE

page 65.   Deindustrialization. Most of this information can be found in John Hughes' most useful book, *Britain in Crisis*, Spokesman, 1981.

page 67F.   Material on the three major responses to poverty can be found in Holman and Townsend (above).

page 68.   Fraser, p. 38 (Chapter Two is a good survey of the Poor Law).

page 70.   Frederick Engels, *The Condition of the Working Class in England*, Panther, 1969; Robert Roberts, *The*

Classic Slum, Pelican, 1973; Graham Markall, *The Best Years of their Lives*, William Temple Foundation, 1980.

page 72.   President Johnson's comments are found in Holman, p. 1. William Cobbett, *Rural Rides*, Penguin, 1977, p. 91.

page 72.   'Family impact statements' are mentioned in Coussins and Coote, (above). Tawney's criteria can be found in his *The Radical Tradition*, Allen & Unwin, 1964, p. 141.

pages 74–5.   National Board for Prices and Incomes, *General Problem of Low Pay*, HMSO, 1971, p. 66. This reference, along with other important information, is in *Low Pay and Poverty in the United Kingdom*, Joan C. Brown, Policy Studies Institute, 1981.

Townsend, p. 63.

page 77.   Tax and national insurance statistics are taken from Frank Field, (above).

page 79.   Lloyd George's thoughts on insurance are in Fraser, pp. 150–7.

pages 80–1.   The toilet story is in Holman, p. 266, and the quotation from Miliband is on p. 274.

page 81.   The Halsey references are in Halsey *Change in British Society*.

CHAPTER SIX

page 91.   Tawney's private papers in the London School of Economics.

pages 91–2.   R.H. Tawney, *The Attack*, Allen & Unwin, 1953, p. 156.

R.H. Tawney, *Equality*, 1952 edition, p. 260.

Tawney, *Equality*, p. 153.

Tawney, *The Radical Tradition*, p. 174.

page 94.   Fabian pamphlet 1943, quoted in Fraser, p. 207.

page 95.   For Piachaud's far more realistic costings of what is needed for living today, see *Children and Poverty*, David Piachaud, Poverty Research Series 9, December 1981, CPAG; and *The Dole*, Centre for Labour Econom-

ics, London School of Economics, Discussion Paper no. 89, May 1981.
page 96.   Tawney's *Equality*, pp. 108, 260, 35–6.

CHAPTER SEVEN

page 103.   *R.H. Tawney's Commonplace Book*, p. 68.
page 110.   *The Guardian*, 19 November 1981; report by Dr. George Moyser, Department of Government, University of Manchester. R.H. Tawney, *The Radical Tradition*, p. 89.
page 110–111.   Dr. E.R. Norman, quoted by Peter Jenkins, *The Guardian*, 17 October 1979. (Norman's Reith Lectures were subsequently published as *Christianity and the World Order*, Oxford University Press, 1979.)
page 112–115.   Four of the five tests of policies are noted in R.H. Preston's *Religion and the Persistence of Capitalism*, SCM, 1979, pp. 48–9. They have been redrafted and a fifth added.
page 114.   Fraser, p. 114.
William Temple, *Christianity and Social Order*, SPCK, 1976 edition, p. 70.
page 118.   R.H. Tawney's papers, London School of Economics.
Further information about 'Church Action on Poverty' can be obtained from its secretary, the Revd Dr John Atherton, William Temple Foundation, Manchester Business School, Manchester M15 6PB.

CONCLUDING NOTE
page 119.   Aneurin Bevan, *In Place of Fear*, Heinemann, 1952.
page 124.   R.H. Tawney, *Equality*, (1964 edition), p. 56.